Measuring Public Relationships

Measuring Public Relationships

The Data-Driven Communicator's
Guide to Success

Katie Delahaye Paine

William T. Paarlberg, editor

KDPaine & Partners
Berlin, New Hampshire

First published in 2007 by
KDPaine & Partners, LLC
177 Main Street
Berlin, NH 03570 USA

ISBN 978-0-9789899-0-3

Cover and text design by Phillip Augusta
Typeset in Palatino

LS
Printed in the United States of America

The paper used in this publication meets the minimum requirements of
the American National Standard for Information Sciences—Permanence of
Paper for Printed Library Materials Z39.48–1992 (R1997).

Contents

Illustrations

Figures

Tables

Foreword

In *Measuring Public Relationships: The Data-Driven Communicator's Guide to Success*, Katie Delahaye Paine has written a book that represents the University of Measurement. We opened the book with great expectations, having known and admired Katie over the years. We closed it understanding a great deal more about both the theory and the nitty-gritty of measurement than when we began.

The book provides a useful appendix of resources that include books and websites, such as that of the Institute for Public Relations Research, dealing with measurement. However, this book alone offers all that most practitioners of public relations will need to satisfy their clients and their own curiosity. It is both current and replete with examples from Katie's rich experience.

Along the way, Katie writes with confidence and transparency. As a result, she helps create the very kind of relationship with readers that she urges them to measure with their publics—a relationship born of trust. For just one example: How many professional communicators—especially those earning a living doing research—remind you that less can be more when conducting a survey? As Katie puts it, "You can probably get most of the information you need from talking to 250 people . . . [s]o don't get talked into surveying thousands if you don't really need to." Good advice, but rare in a world where commercial firms may charge by the numbers.

Katie also provides cogent and concise explanations of the often arcane world of measurement and evaluation. In the above example, she explains that it's possible to survey a mere 500 people and get a representative sample of the whole population of the United States. Thus the book speaks to novices and veterans of the world of measurement.

Throughout, Katie emphasizes the importance of measuring relationships. In this way alone, she sets her book apart from many others—those that focus on media hits, for example, or strategic messaging. She clearly differentiates among measuring outputs, outtakes, and outcomes. She proceeds from one strategic public to another, not assuming that one system of measurement fits all. So she describes how to measure relationships with the community, opinion leaders, employees, members, investors, partners, the media, and sales reps. She teases out what is unique about evaluating relationships in times of crisis and through blogs. She tells how to plan and budget. She does all this through both words and figures, exactly as a competent research report would be prepared.

In *Measuring Public Relationships*, Katie Paine walks the walk that so many of her colleagues merely talk about. The typical book on research, like too many researchers, over-promises and under-delivers. Readers, anxious to know more and to do better, approach these books with optimism but leave in frustration at the level of the text or its inadequate explication. At the very least, their minds feel chloroformed by the language.

By contrast, here we have a book that is a lively, engaging, accessible, wise, and candid reflection of all Katie has done and learned. Her legacy in this book of accumulated wisdom is guaranteed. It is such a remarkable compendium that it almost makes us wish we hadn't retired, so we could assign it as required reading in every single class.

Larissa A. Grunig
James E. Grunig
Professors Emeriti
Department of Communication
University of Maryland

Preface

We talk about the quality of product and service. What about the quality of our relationships, and the quality of our communications and the quality of our promises to each other?
— Max De Pree

Once upon a time not very long ago, there was a state university in a small town in New England. Both the university and the town needed new soccer fields. One of the university's alumni, a successful local entrepreneur, stepped forward and offered to donate $6 million so the university could build them. A site was selected, town officials were notified, and the university assumed it would soon be hosting soccer tournaments.

Now the university was a venerable institution, and it took care to maintain its reputation of quality and prestige by communicating about itself to the world. But it failed to understand that some very important changes had been occurring in the town. For much of the university's history, most of the people who lived in the town year round either worked for the university, or had family or friends involved there. Over recent decades, however, rising real estate prices and property taxes had forced much of the faculty and staff out of town. Their houses were bought up by retirees and commuters who had no particular connection with the university. So the town's permanent residents, who had once formed a sympathetic constituency, gradually changed into an inactive, disengaged public. The university's reputation with this new public was still fine, but the strength of its connection with them was now different—unmeasured and untested.

Several years before the soccer fields were planned, the university had embarked on a different large construction project, a 6,000-seat sports and entertainment arena. The university, a tax-exempt and local zoning-exempt state entity, chose to simply notify the townspeople of their plans. It completely failed to anticipate that the town's permanent residents might object to potential parking problems or the absence of any local tax benefits. As a result, many townspeople felt railroaded by the university and their town officials, and, after a contentious political campaign, replaced the town leadership.

Let's skip ahead a couple of years to the soccer fields proposal. The university, despite its strong public relations department, had been making no effort to understand the concerns of its constituencies. It was unaware that a good part of the town's permanent residents had become well-organized and were potentially quite hostile. When the university announced their new construction project, the reaction was swift, noisy, and disastrous. The citizens' group, now 2000 members strong, got the attention of the statewide media, and used email and their listserve to ensure that every university trustee and every politician heard their complaints.

Less than two months after being announced, the proposed soccer fields were cancelled, the $6-million gift was rejected, and the university president stepped down. It was a stiff price to pay for misunderstanding one's publics. What went wrong?

Some argue that the university should have just paid more attention to its PR. And it should have. But the missing concept here is more complex than communications, or even reputation. What the university failed to understand or evaluate was the mutual affinity that existed (or did not) between itself and the townspeople. It failed to understand its *relationship* with them.

※   ※   ※

Those of us in communications and marketing have all felt an increased demand for more relevant and accurate measures of success. Slogans like "If you can't measure it, you can't manage it" adorn offices around the globe, and everyone who communicates for a living is feeling pressure to demonstrate just how they are helping advance their organization's mission.

For almost two decades I've studied and measured communications programs for organizations. Many of those were based in public relations or media relations. Others were focused on employee communications or events or trade shows. I've figured out how to measure successes in many shapes and forms. The one common denominator in all those programs has been relationships—lots of different types of relationships with lots of different constituencies.

In many organizations, marketing and communications is seen as a tool to improve corporate or brand reputation. And, while most of us in the PR business are convinced that it does contribute, trying to tie a specific activity back to overall brand reputation tends to be a frustrating and time-consuming experience, undertaken mostly by large organizations with hefty research budgets. I am convinced that the key to understanding reputation is measuring the relationships that it is based on.

Whether you work for a Fortune 500 international powerhouse or run a local nonprofit, you share a common interest in the relationships you have with your constituencies. Building, managing, and measuring those relationships are fundamental to your success and the success of your organization.

As our world has become more electronic and in many ways less personal, the importance of those relationships has increased. Our new and efficient communication technologies sometimes operate to the detriment of relationships both interpersonal and organizational. For some organizations, understanding how to measure and better manage their relationships is becoming a matter of survival. If you can measure your relationships you can improve them, and improved relationships will bring you and your organization increased efficiencies, greater effectiveness, and improved overall performance.

This book has grown from my experience in designing and implementing measurement systems. It is based on hundreds of actual stories about how organizations have used measurement to improve their reputations, strengthen their bottom lines, and improve efficiencies all around. The following pages provide you with tools, tips, techniques, and experiences that illustrate how to measure your success, and specifically the success of your relationships. This is a book that every professional communicator can use—whether he or she works for Procter & Gamble or for a small, local nonprofit—to improve their work and the organization they work for.

Here's wishing you great measures of success,

—*Katie Delahaye Paine*

Chapter 1

An Introduction to Measurement

I can think of nothing more gallant, even though again and again we fail, than attempting to get at the facts; attempting to tell things as they really are. For at least reality, though never fully attained, can be defined. Reality is that which, when you don't believe in it, doesn't go away.
—Peter Viereck

Let's be perfectly clear. If all you want to do is measure your media relations program, you can skip ahead to Chapter 3. But that's not what public relations measurement is all about. Too often those of us who consider ourselves PR professionals forget that the second word in our title is "relations," as in the relationships you have with various publics. PR is the process of building and enhancing relationships with key constituencies. Particularly in this day and age where conversations with stakeholders are critical to your survival, the importance of good relationships with key publics can't be underestimated.

How This Book Is Organized:
A Practical Guide to Hands-On Measurement

PR measurement is a multi-disciplinary combination of communications, research methods, statistics, social psychology, and office politics. This book adds the study of human relationships to the mix—a theme that's always been present, but that is now far more accessible thanks to the recent development of practical survey techniques for measuring relationships.

Despite its complex foundations, PR measurement involves, above all, hands-on research. It is the practical aspect of actually doing that research that is the focus of this book. To that end most of its chapters are organized around three aspects of measurement programs: the Seven Basic Steps, the stakeholders, and outputs, outtakes and outcomes.

The Seven Basic Steps of Any Measurement Program

Public relations measurement is a circular, reiterative process in which information is acquired and then changes are made based on that information, and then more information is acquired, and more changes are made, and so on again and again. Most measurement programs, no matter what the stakeholders or metrics, proceed through this process with seven basic logical steps. These Seven Basic Steps are discussed at length later in this chapter, and they form the framework for most of the chapters to follow. Once you are familiar with these steps, you can adapt them to any measurement program you encounter.

Stakeholders

While every PR program is different, all professional communicators have a core set of key publics that they need to build relationships with, collectively known as the stakeholders. These include, among others: the media, employees, customers, distributors or sales force, the local community, and elected officials. Each stakeholder group requires slightly different measurement tools and slightly different metrics. That's why this book is organized around the stakeholders—each with its own chapter and its own procedures and advice. When you're done reading this book, you'll know how to measure relationships with just about any key public that your job involves.

Outputs, Outtakes and Outcomes

This book is also organized around the three categories of the results of public relations efforts: outputs, outtakes, and outcomes. Outputs are the physical results (like clippings or brochures), outtakes are how people think as a result of experiencing the outputs (typically measured with a survey), and outcomes are how people behave as a result of the outputs (like buying or recommending a product). Each stakeholder chapter includes a list of the most useful output, outtake, and outcome metrics for programs directed at those stakeholders.

We will return to the practical aspects of actually doing measurement later in this chapter. First, however, it is important to understand how and why relationships are a vital component of public relations and its measurement.

Measuring Relationships versus Measuring Reputation

Over the last decade, people have been focussing a lot of attention on the measurement and evaluation of corporate reputation. While investors, shareholders, and management consultants are all legitimately concerned with reputation, I hold that evaluating your reputation is largely a waste of time. Just because you can measure it, does *not* mean you can manage it. Sure, you can count the number of times the media mention your company as a good place to work, or as socially responsible. But if you are mishandling the relationships behind your reputation, all those messages are not grounded in reality, and ultimately you will have a problem on your hands.

As Grunig, Grunig, and Dozier said in *Excellent Public Relations and Effective Organizations*:

> [W]e show that the value of public relations comes from the relationships that communicators develop and maintain with publics. We show that reputation is a product of relationships and that the quality of relationships and

reputation result more from the behavior of the organization than from the messages that communicators disseminate.

The difficulty with reputation measurement is that it is an overly simplistic look at corporate relationships. As you will see in the chapters ahead, relationships between an organization and its publics are made up of several independent and measurable components. If you want to have a prayer of influencing your reputation, you first need to understand and measure the relationships behind it.

That measurement can take a number of forms. The simplest and least costly might be an analysis of local and regional blogs to see what people are saying. The traditional media are also a good bellwether of local sentiment. To truly quantify the health of your relationships, however, you will need to conduct a statistically valid survey based on the Grunig Relationship Survey (see Appendix 1).

It almost always makes good economic sense to continuously measure your relationships. Healthy relationships pay off in reduced legal fees, lower turnover, higher customer loyalty, and greater efficiencies. And bad relationships are costly in the extreme.

Consider the example I gave in the Preface, of the university and the small town. The irony there is that the university is home to a prestigious business school, known for its polling and survey capabilities. The cost to actually measure town/gown relationships would have been minimal. And compared to the loss of a $6-million gift, the return on investment (ROI) would have been off the charts.

Measure Relationships to Manage Reputation

Because the reputation of your company or organization is a product of all of your relationships with all your constituencies, managing those relationships effectively is the key to a successful public relations program. And you can't manage relationships unless you measure them.

As warm and fuzzy as it might sound, relationships are highly measurable. The breakthrough work of Drs. James and Laurie Grunig and Dr. Linda Hon has provided working definitions of what relationships are and proven survey methodologies to measure them. In this book, you will learn how the Grunig survey, combined with media analysis and other tools, provides the means to measure and understand relationships with each of your constituencies.

Outtakes and outcomes can also be measures of relationships. (See the Glossary for definitions of outputs, outtakes, and outputs, each a product of public relations programs.) In a good relationship, one person "takes away" from an interaction the feeling or perception that the other wants them to have. In a bad relationship, one person ignores the other, or thinks differently. For outcomes, if people have a good relationship, then they behave in ways that are mutually beneficial.

Relationships and Organizational Excellence

In the IABC Excellence Study (see the IABC website http://www.iabc.com/rf/reports.htm), Grunig, Grunig, and Dozier conclusively showed that the role of public relations in truly excellent companies was to manage relationships between the organization and its key constituencies. The more an organization focused on relationships, the more "excellent" the organization was.

That's all well and good in theory, and I truly believe that most CEOs do fund corporate communications departments with that in mind, but many of the corporate communications people we've interviewed in the last decade inevitably say that they are paid to do something very different, starting with "get good press," followed by "get my CEO's name in print," "keep us out of the headlines," "communicate our message," and so on.

If you start with a misunderstanding about goals between top management and the front-line practitioners, measurement will never reflect the goals of the organization, no matter how or what you measure. So if excellent companies need excellent corporate communications departments, and excellent corporate communications departments are focused on managing relationships, clearly the 50-plus percent of corporate communications departments that are now measuring success by column inches need to change their measures of success. This is why we are seeing more organizations moving from simple media metrics, such as clip counts and column inches, to more sophisticated reputation and relationship measures. It's not that one type of measure is inherently better than the other; it's that if you don't incorporate and integrate the output measures with the outcome measures, you will never truly understand what impact you are having on your organization.

Why Measure at All?

When budgets are flush, it doesn't much matter how you measure results, as long as there is a perfunctory number that shows up next to your department every so often. But times aren't always flush, and the bean counters are getting more demanding.

Today, most professional communicators have heard the call for accountability, yet few know how to answer it. The standard response a dozen years ago was (to twist a quote from John Wanamaker), "I know half of my communications is working, I just don't know which half." To say that communications is intangible or too "warm and fuzzy" to be measured is no longer an acceptable answer, and that is why an increasing number of communications professionals struggle to figure out what to measure and how to fit measurement and evaluation into already tight budgets.

I entered the field of corporate communications via journalism, so I had little practical knowledge of communications tactics and strategies. I asked a lot of questions, such as where we got the most bang for the buck or which strategy resulted in the cheapest cost per message communicated. Since no one seemed to have the answers at their fingertips, I developed systems to get the data. Those systems are described in detail in the following chapters.

But along the way I learned that measuring your success is not just another buzzword that follows Six Sigma, TQM (Total Quality Management), and paradigm shifts. It is a key strategic tool that helps you better manage your resources, your department, and your career. There are half a dozen advantages to setting up a measurement program no matter where you are.

Data-Driven PR Rules

Making decisions based on data saves time and boosts your credibility. When faced with tough decisions, you'll seldom find your board of directors or CEO relying on hunches or gut instinct. Chances are any decisions made at the highest level of your company will be made following extensive research.

So why should public relations and/or corporate communications be any different? How credible would your CFO be if he got up in front of the board and said, "I know we're making money because I see checks coming in?"

Just as the CFO relies on data to give advice and make recommendations, you need data to decide where, when, and how to allocate resources.

It Helps Preserve Budget and Staff

I once used a competitive media analysis to indicate the need for a PR staff for a major semiconductor company. We analyzed the client's presence in key media compared to those of three competitors to determine who was earning the greatest share of ink. As it happened, over a two-year period there was very little difference between the competitors, with each of the four organizations earning about 25 percent share of ink each month. But at a certain point the client's results took a dive; all of a sudden its share of ink dropped to about 2 percent. I presented the results and asked the audience, which included several managers, what had happened. The answer: "That was when we reorganized and eliminated our PR effort."

I replied by demonstrating that, in the months following the reorganization, the market had had about nine times more opportunities to see news about the competition's products than their own. That seemed to do the trick; the last time I was in touch, the PR staff had grown to about ten people and their budget was increasing every year.

Gain a Better Understanding of the Competition

Whether you are competing for share of market, share of wallet, or share of voice, in today's fast-paced environment you need to know how you stack up against your peers and rivals. Measurement gives you insight into competitive strengths and weaknesses.

Strategic Planning

Deciding how to best allocate resources is arguably the most important responsibility of any communications manager. But without data you are forced to rely on gut instinct. And as accurate as your gut may be, it doesn't translate very well into numbers. Besides, you and your gut and all of your persuasive abilities aren't going to do anyone any good if you are not in the boardroom where budgets get decided. What you need is data, data that tells you where and how to communicate key messages, to impact your reputation, and to effect outcomes. Only with such data can you most effectively allocate your resources.

Measurement Reveals Strengths and Weaknesses

Measurement isn't something you should do because you're forced to. It should be approached as an essential, strategic tool to more effectively get your messages out. Deciding how to

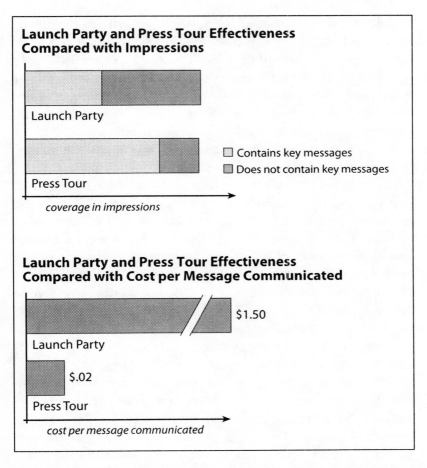

Launch Party and Press Tour Effectiveness Compared with Impressions

Launch Party

Press Tour

□ Contains key messages
▣ Does not contain key messages

coverage in impressions

Launch Party and Press Tour Effectiveness Compared with Cost per Message Communicated

$1.50

Launch Party

$.02

Press Tour

cost per message communicated

Figure 1. Media analysis is one way to demonstrate what works and what doesn't.

allocate the necessary resources and staff is easier if you know exactly what works and what doesn't.

One of my first experiences with measurement was at Lotus Development (now IBM Software). I was nearing the end of my first year there and wanted to determine what had worked and what hadn't. My primary role was to insure the successful communication of key messages to the target audience. So we gathered the 2,400 or so articles that mentioned Lotus during the previous year and analyzed each one to determine whether it left a reader more or less likely to purchase Lotus software, and whether it contained one or more of the key messages our company was trying to communicate about itself. Since I was clearly too close to the process and could spot a key message a mile away, I hired a twenty-something college student who was in the market for software to analyze each article.

The results were very revealing. The $350,000 launch (with a major cocktail party) of a word processing product generated plenty of coverage, but very few of those articles contained our key messages. In fact, a $15,000 press tour was much more effective at getting key messages to our target audiences. The metric we used to measure success was cost per message communicated (CPMC), and the press tour delivered a CPMC of $.02 compared to the party's CPMC of $1.50 (see Figure 1, page 9).

Even more revealing was when we looked at our success in penetrating new markets. We were targeting software buyers with a product that required us to reach an entirely new group of journalists. When we analyzed the results, we realized that this new group of journalists had not responded well at all to our pitch, and in fact their stories were only half as likely to contain key messages. I called a few of these journalists, tracked down the source of their problem, and eventually resolved the difficulty.

Another example involved a client who had us compare the results of two separate press introductions—a press tour and a press conference—to determine which technique was more effective. The results varied little in terms of quantity. In terms of quality, however, the press tour received nearly twice as much positive press and communicated almost twice as many messages, all for a fraction of the cost of the press conference. I showed my client a chart similar to the one in Figure 2, page 11, to demonstrate unequivocally that press

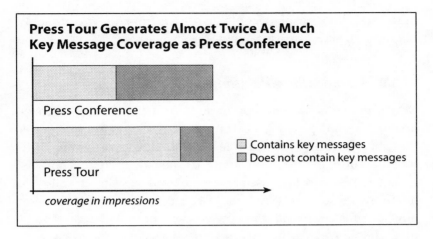

Press Tour Generates Almost Twice As Much Key Message Coverage as Press Conference

Press Conference

Press Tour

☐ Contains key messages
▨ Does not contain key messages

coverage in impressions

Figure 2. Use charts like this to demonstrate what works and what doesn't.

tours were more effective than press conferences at getting messages across and generating articles that leave readers more likely to purchase the product.

Measurement Gives You Reasons to Say "No"

All too often, making decisions based on gut feeling rather than data leads to overworked communicators with unclear priorities. There is simply no good argument for which to say "No." However, if you can study the results of programs for which timing was rushed, or materials were not prepared far enough in advance, you frequently gain the ammunition necessary to be able to turn down requests that will be a waste of time or resources.

Dispelling the Myths of Measurement

So if accountability is all that important, why isn't everyone already measuring? There are a number of bona fide reasons—lack of knowledge, lack of time, lack of a clear strategy—but most of the so-called reasons people give stem from a few commonly held myths about measurement.

Myth: Measurement = Punishment

Measurement is not a weapon that your manager uses to check up on you and justify punishing you. Not only are you never punished for being accountable, in fact, most people who institute measurement programs find that they get more promotions, bigger raises, and increased budgets because of their ability to demonstrate success. Why would you be punished for showing how to make your program more efficient, or for having clear and quantifiable ways to figure out what works or doesn't work?

Myth: Measurement Will Only Create More Work for Me

I realize that in the overall scheme of things, measurement seems to many of us just one more thing in a long list of high priority items. Too often it gets dropped to the bottom of the priority list because it seems like too much work. The reality is that once a measurement system is in place, it actually makes everything else much easier.

Data at your fingertips saves time in deciding what media outlets to target, and it saves resources by showing clearly which weaknesses need to be addressed immediately. It helps you better direct the resources you have, ensuring that their efforts are having maximum impact. Data at your disposal means less time debating the merits of one tactic over another. Gut feelings can always be second guessed, but data is much harder to argue with.

Myth: Measurement Is Expensive

The number one reason that people give for not measuring is that they can't afford it. The truth is, you cannot afford *not* to measure. Without measurement, you have no way of knowing which tactics work, and whether you spent your dollars effectively. A measurement system frequently pays for itself because it inevitably leads to increased efficiency.

One international client of ours called its PR agencies together and showed them the results of our benchmark measurement study of their PR. Based on those results, the agencies were given concise new objectives for directing specific messages to specific audiences. Six months later, the percentage of the company's articles that contained key messages had risen by 245 percent. Think of that: A tool that could more than double the exposure of key messages to your target audience. If our client had attempted to gain that exposure with advertising, it would have paid close to $100,000; instead, the measurement program cost them less than $10,000.

Myth: Measurement Is Strictly Quantitative

Another myth claims that measurement primarily concerns quantifiable entities, such as numbers, column inches, total opportunities to see, and so forth. The reality, however, is that the only type of measurement system that works combines both qualitative and quantitative data. Increasing your press coverage is useless unless the right people see it and it communicates the messages you intend.

Myth: Measurement Is Something You Do When a Program Is Over

Measurement is seen too frequently as an afterthought, a tool to gauge the efficiency of a program you have already completed. On the contrary, in order to be an effective planning tool, measurement should be in place at the start of a program.

Myth: "I Know What's Going on Because I See Clips Coming In."

"I know what's happening; I don't need research." The reality is that you need formal systems to track and evaluate your entire program. Without them you will only be judged on your last headline.

So repeat after me and make measurement your mantra: "Measurement is good. Measurement will not hurt me. Measurement will get me that big raise I've been dreaming about." Repeat five times, then read on.

Ten Questions Every Communications Professional Must Be Able to Answer

The first thing you need to do in order to build internal support and engagement around your measurement program is to walk around your organization, and check in with the research groups, customer relations departments, and anywhere there might be internal data that can be used to measure success. Then, make sure you have the answers to the following ten basic questions that any professional communicator should know. If you don't have the answers at your fingertips, go get them.

1. *What are your corporate objectives?* You must start with a thorough understanding of your company or organization's business objectives. And if they are not written down somewhere, ask your boss; you might have a very interesting conversation.

2. *What are your department objectives?* While it may seem facile and simplistic to actually put this question on the list, it is amazing how many communications professionals I've met with who cannot answer it. Or if they can answer, the objectives are not measurable.

   I sometimes help them through the process by asking them to shut their eyes and imagine that it is the end of the year, and they are celebrating enormous success— corks are popping, champagne is flowing, and bonus checks are being passed out to everyone. What is it that they are celebrating? Another way to define your mission is to frame it from the opposite perspective. Suppose your department was wiped out tomorrow, how would the business suffer?

3. *What are you going to do with the information you get from your research?* Never ask a question you don't want to hear the answer to. Make sure you can act on all the information you get and can make changes and improve performance as a result. If your report is going to the CEO, you have 20 seconds or less to get your message across, so your report must make an impact like that of a billboard. If it is going to marketing, the report should be short, but detailed enough to include brand data as well as corporate data. If it is for market research, you'll need to provide cross tabs and other supporting data. If it's for the vice president of communications, you'll want to make sure you go into a bit more detail as to why certain results are the way they are.

4. *What other departments/areas will be affected?* Or, who will be involved in implementing changes as a result of your measurement program? This is one of the most important questions, because if you do not have buy-in from all departments to change their behavior or strategy, then your measurement program will be a waste of effort. Whoever might have to change as a result of your measurement needs to be involved in the process of designing the measurement program. Without buy-in, change will not happen.

5. *What are your key messages?* If you haven't articulated them yet, or don't know what they are, do research to figure out what messages will resonate most forcefully with your target audience.

6. *Who are your program's target audience(s)?* This is another question that may be pretty obvious for some companies,

but it never hurts to get it in writing. The important thing to do is to define the audience as specifically as you can. No matter what you sell, the answer to this question is not, "Anyone with a pulse." There is always, within any market, a set of customers who are the most profitable, the most valuable. These are the ones you want to target.

7. *Who influences that audience?* You need to look at what all the influences are on that audience: websites, online publications, politicians, nongovernmental organizations, peers, educators, discussion groups, industry gurus, and so on.

8. *How do you distribute your product or service?* Who are the secondary influences on your business? These are sometimes equally important to your efforts to effect change.

9. *What measurement programs are currently underway?* You may be able to tailor new measures to complement existing ones. For instance, could sales or lead tracking data be compared to PR activities and measures?

10. *What's important to your audiences?* Once you've defined the profile, you can go about determining what issues matter most to the audience: What inspires them? What scares them? What are they most passionate about? Where do they go for information? All of our research shows that the closer you get to a person's passions, the more likely they are to be loyal to your company or brand.

What's important about this Ten Questions exercise is not so much knowing the right answers as it is achieving consensus among the people who will be using and/or contributing to the measurement data. Getting everyone on the same page is an absolute necessity before you can begin to implement a measurement program.

The Seven Basic Steps of Any Measurement Program

As I mentioned earlier, public relations measurement is a logical, circular process of adjustment and improvement. Information is acquired, changes are made based on that information, and then more information is acquired, and more changes are made, and so on again and again. Most measurement programs, no matter what the stakeholders or metrics, proceed through this process with seven basic steps. We'll talk about each of them here in detail.

Step 1: Identify the Audiences and Publics with Whom You Have Relationships

Every organization continuously communicates with numerous audiences, including the media, prospects, customers, partners, employees, governments, communities, investors, thought leaders, and the international community. While you may think your advertising and public relations are reaching only your customers and your prospects, in reality it may be seen by your other audiences, too. And with the help of the Internet, most of the time you communicate to those same audiences around the world.

The best way to identify and agree on just who your own audiences are is to put all the communications people in your organization in a room and ask them. You may be surprised by the answers. When doing this I've sometimes ended up with two dozen distinct audiences. Get as many as possible down on paper and then ask them to prioritize the list.

Step 2: Define Objectives for Each Audience

You can't start to measure success until you know what success means for you. So, the next question you need to ask the group is: How does a good relationship with each audience benefit the organization and how might a bad relationship threaten it? Articulate what are the specific benefits of your efforts. The answers should relate back to strategic corporate goals, such as increasing market share, owning a position in the marketplace, or, for nonprofits, fulfilling a mission.

To help people clarify their objectives, we surveyed corporate communications professionals to see what they thought was the most important objective for their PR program. Eighty-five percent cited product or corporate awareness.

Other typical objectives included the following:

- Increase exposure for the company name or product

- Increase dissemination of company or product messages

- Educate certain publics

- Generate leads

- Move prospects along the purchase cycle

- Sell product

Once these larger goals are set—and at least one should be set for each audience—you can then prioritize your efforts according to which benefits are most important to your organization. Force rank each audience, no ties allowed!

Now, starting with the most important goals and audiences, set specific and measurable objectives. And be sure they include a time frame. For example: "Achieve 25 percent more awareness of product than the competition by the end of the fourth quarter."

A typical problem occurs when groups have mixed objectives. For example, one of the most frequently mentioned goals we hear is, "To reach our target audiences with our key quality message." This goal is great as long as the target audiences are similar. But what if one product group is targeting seniors and the next is targeting college students? Quality may mean different things to different audiences. The best solution here is to create separate objectives for each specific population.

Step 3: Define Your Measurement Criteria

Once you've agreed upon your objectives, you must establish the specific criteria of success that you will measure. Each objective may require a different type of measurement. Some criteria are tied to output measures, like getting messages out to a particular audience. Others may be outtake measures, like raising awareness for your brand. And still others may be outcome measures, like getting people to attend your event, or download something from your website. If your objective is awareness, the criterion might be the percentage increase of unaided awareness. If your objective is to sell product, the criterion might be the incremental sales after a particular PR or promotional program took place.

Years of advertising research indicates that visibility is directly linked to awareness. So if awareness is your objective, it is critical that your publicity programs break through the clutter and get your name out more prominently than the competition. This doesn't just mean more articles. It means more mentions of the company name in headlines, captions, and other places of greater visibility.

The criterion for success in this case could be sheer volume of coverage compared to the competition. An even better measure would be percent of articles featuring the company name in the headline. This figure would then be compared to the percent of articles that mention the competition's name in the headlines. That data could then be compared to ongoing brand awareness tracking studies to compare the impact of your earned media with that of your paid media.

A common element of publicity programs is to establish company spokespeople as industry leaders or reliable sources on topics of interest. In this case a goal could be to boost your share of quotes to be equal to or greater than that of the competition by some particular point in time. Obviously if your spokesperson is getting quoted more often than the owner of a competitive franchise, then your program is more effective.

Goals, Actions, and Metrics

Goals	Message Consistency	Employee Engagement	Implementation of Customer-centric Program
Actions	Develop tools and vehicles: website, newsletter, posters, talking points	Conversations with management	Programs promoting Customer First, bulletins, posters, roundtables
Output Metrics	- Did they publish on time? - How many people saw it? - How many people requested or downloaded it?	How many emails containing key messages were sent out?	How many communiqués occurred around customer centricity?
Outtake Metrics	- Percent hearing message - Percent believing message	- Percent who know about engagement programs - Percent who believe engagement messages	- Percent aware of customer program - Percent understanding customer program
Outcome Metrics	- Percent consistency in messaging between external and internal communications - Percent employees correctly answering test question	- Percent increase in recommending as a good place to work - Percent lower turnover rate - Number of referrals	- Improved customer satisfaction - Revenue per employee - Improved employee performance scores

Table 1. Laying out your goals, actions, and metrics will help you define your measurement criteria.

One thing I've learned by studying hundreds of communication programs is that quality has no single definition. Different aspects of communication are important to different people. Table 1 presents a variety of possible actions and metrics that could be appropriate for three typical program goals. Criteria and metrics that are best for your particular measurement program

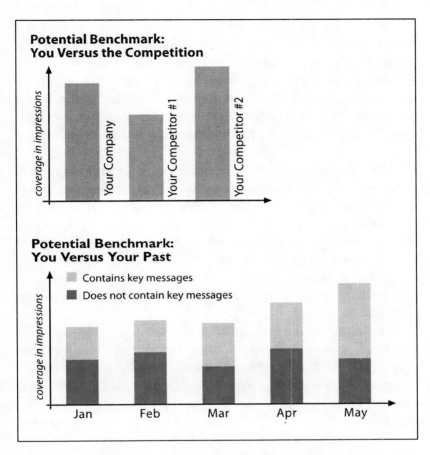

Figure 3. The above graphs demonstrate two typical benchmarks and how you would work with them. It's important that you define benchmarks appropriate to your company's goals.

will depend on many factors. We'll be discussing specific criteria appropriate for different audiences over the next few chapters.

Step 4: Define Your Benchmark

The key point to remember about any evaluation program is that measurement is a comparative tool; to decide if you are successful you compare your results to something else. The most effective comparisons are to your competition and peers over time, to just yourself over time, or to an industry average.

Ideally you would benchmark against two or three competitors: a stretch goal, a peer company, and an underdog who's just beginning to nip at your heels (see Figure 3, page 21). Remember, even if you're in the nonprofit sector, you are still competing for share of wallet.

The next most effective benchmark is to compare your company to its past performance over time. If possible, don't just arbitrarily pick a calendar year or quarter; choose your benchmark(s) so you can track the results of a significant event, such as when a new CEO joined the company or when a new agency signed on. While this will tell you how your performance is improving or declining, it won't tell you anything about how you are doing relative to the market. If at all possible, track your competitors, too.

The least expensive benchmark is an industry survey. If you're a big enough company, these benchmark studies can be particularly useful. I conducted one study with over a hundred thousand articles analyzed over several years and found that, on average, 30 percent of all articles were positive, 6 percent were negative and 29 percent communicated key messages. However, the actual numbers vary considerably between business-to-business and consumer organizations.

Step 5: Select a Measurement Tool

Your measurement tools are the techniques you will use to collect data. Remember that these are useless unless they collect the sort of data that will help you evaluate your progress toward your goals. Essentially, you will be collecting data in one of these three ways:

1. Primary research via telephone, mail, or online survey

2. Secondary research of other data available

3. Primary research in the media, including Internet sources

Measurement tools are covered in detail in Chapter 2.

Not only do your tools need to collect the right data, they must be affordable and provide the data when you need it. At one company I worked for we did all of our planning in August, yet the yearly benchmark evaluation of our PR program occurred in January. Thus the data we worked with while planning was six months out of date. And the new data wouldn't be available until the following January, giving rise to the oft-repeated groan, "If we only had the analysis now." "On time" for most companies means that you have a report in hand when it is of value, that is, as you start your planning.

Step 6: Analyze Data, Draw Actionable Conclusions, and Make Recommendations

The most important element in any measurement program is the analysis of the data to arrive at valid, actionable conclusions. Once you've collected all of your results, avoid the temptation to focus only on the most exciting. I've seen many reports gloat that, "Press coverage increased by 50 percent!" but fail to mention that reach into the highest priority audience segment dropped by 15 percent or that the key messages about a particular product were never communicated.

To make information meaningful and actionable, relate each conclusion back to your original objectives. Compare the length of your message communication bar this quarter to its length last quarter. As a history major working in engineering companies, I quickly learned that the key to action was to communicate with my top management in language they could understand. The language of business is charts and graphs. Therefore, to put measurement to work for you, you must learn to translate your raw

Leverage the Value of Your Measurement Efforts

You will never be as powerful or persuasive as when you present your results to your bosses, so plan your presentation according to what actions you might want them to take:

- **Ask for Money.** Many clients I've worked with have asked for and received additional budgetary dollars immediately after presenting their results, just on the strength of their measurement programs and insights.
- **Get Commitment.** Have you ever had a hard time persuading an executive to go on a press tour? Show them a chart to indicate the potential disaster if they don't go.
- **Manage Timing.** To demonstrate how effective strategic timing can be, present your results in graphs and charts that show changes over time.
- **Buy Influence.** Use your results to win other departments over to your point of view and approve your programs.
- **Get Outside Help.** You may want to convince your bosses that you need more help to achieve the results they desire. One of our client's coverage skyrocketed in August and continued at vastly increased rates. I couldn't figure out what happened, until I learned that the client had doubled its staff in July.
- **Just Say No.** By using your results to demonstrate what doesn't work, you can frequently dissuade managers and colleagues from repeating mistakes. Has a product manager ever asked you to do a party or a press conference just because it would be, "A fun way to introduce the product?" Say "No" by showing the manager a chart demonstrating that a press tour communicates your key messages much more effectively.

numbers into charts and graphs with short headlines that draw conclusions from the data. Once you've done so, you're one step closer to actionable information.

The other aspect of ensuring that your information is actionable is applying it to relevant programs that you can do something about. Do not measure dead products, competitors that aren't viable, or publications you don't have time to target.

Step 7: Make Changes and Measure Again

At its core, measurement is a continuous improvement process. For any measurement system to work, you need to assess results, make changes, see if those changes had an impact, make more changes, and so on.

Ideally, whenever you need to decide what tactic to use, what resources to pull in, or what spokesperson or message to emphasize, you will have up-to-date data at your fingertips. For that reason you need to set up a regular reporting schedule so that in addition to demonstrating results, you can also get buy-in to changes in the program.

Chapter 2

Measurement Tools and What They Cost

Whenever you can, count.
—Francis Galton

Measurement tools and systems have advanced tremendously in the last decade or so. Gathering data, whether from media outlets or customers, becomes faster and cheaper every year, and new measurement tools and techniques are developed all the time. It's beyond the scope of this book to cover all of them, but this chapter will give you a good introduction to most of those mentioned elsewhere in this book.

While the fundamental techniques of statistics and research design don't change much, the ability of new technologies to get interesting data (sometimes too much of it) into our hands does change rapidly. Electronic access to data from thousands of media outlets combined with automated content analysis has revolutionized the clipping and content analysis business. You can now get daily analysis of your clips delivered to your desktop 24/7.

Another example of how high technology is affecting measurement is interactive phone sampling. If you watched the 2004 presidential debates you saw this technique in action. A sample of voters was polled and constituency reaction to the candidates' statements was recorded via the voters' phone lines. Technology in the form of store checkout scanners now makes tracking sales impact far easier than ever before. Colgate Palmolive uses scanned sell-through data to track the specific profitability (ROI) of any given promotion on a brand-by-brand basis.

The only way to stay on top of this change is to continually educate yourself. A good place to start is at the Institute for Public Relations website, www.instituteforpr.org. Another good resource is www.measuresofsuccess.com, a measurement resource clear-inghouse that my company, KDPaine & Partners, operates. See Appendix 2 for a list of educational resources.

The Right Tools for the Job

Even the most sophisticated measurement tool is worthless if it can't measure progress toward your goals. If your goal is aware-ness, for instance, no amount of simple clip counting will tell you if you are achieving it. You must use some technique that will measure the degree to which your publics are aware of your brand, your brand benefits, or your messages. See Table 2, page 29, for some examples of program objectives, typical metrics for measuring those objectives, tools to gather the data, and sample vendors to supply those tools. These are just a few examples from the great many options available; what you actually use will depend on the details of your program.

There are two ways to get data on your target audience: directly and indirectly. Direct data comes from surveys, focus groups, and chat rooms on the Internet. Indirect data can be retrieved from secondary sources, such as syndicated industry sources and the media.

Ultimately you will want to establish a system that mea-sures your processes, your outputs (Did your messages get out there?), your outtakes (What did your publics take away from your efforts?), as well as your outcomes (see the Glossary for more detailed definitions of these concepts). Combining a variety of measurement tools is the best approach to looking at the big picture impact of what you do.

The Right Tools for the Job

Objective	Metric	The Right Tool and Sample Vendors
- **inquiries** - **web traffic** - **recruitment**	- percent increase in traffic - clickthroughs or downloads	web server analytics, e.g., Clicktrax or WebTrends
preference	- percent of audience preferring your brand to the competition	online surveys, e.g., SurveyMonkey or Zoomerang
awareness	- percent awareness of your product - cost per impression	online surveys, e.g., SurveyMonkey or Zoomerang
communicate messages	- percent of articles containing key messages - total opportunities to see key messages - cost per opportunity to see key messages	media analysis, e.g., Clipmetrics, DIY Dashboard, Cymfony, Biz360, Vocus, MediaSense, Echo or CARMA
	- percent aware of or believing in key messages	surveys

Table 2. You must select measurement tools that can best measure your goals.

Because many organizations and budgets can't accommodate instant implementation of a full scale measurement program, we'll start with some very basic tools and work upward from there.

Opinion Research and Surveys

If your objectives are to increase product or service awareness or preference, or your goal is to educate an audience, you need

Qualitative and Quantitative Research

Focus Groups Provide Insight

Focus groups can help you probe to discover the real issues that concern people. If the major messages aren't getting through, what is? It is important to keep in mind that qualitative research (e.g., focus groups, one-on-one in-depth interviews, convenience polling) is usually open-ended, free response and unstructured in format. It generally relies on nonrandom samples and its results are rarely generalizable to larger audiences.

Surveys Provide Facts, Polls Provide Data

Although it may contain some open-ended questions, quantitative research (e.g., telephone, mail, mall, Internet, fax, and email polls) is far more apt to involve the use of closed-ended, forced-choice questions, that are highly structured in format. It generally relies on random samples and usually is projectable to larger audiences.

The truth is that measurement involves numbers and, ultimately, charts and graphs to display those numbers. These tools make up the language of management; when you start talking benchmarking, the vocabulary becomes statistics.

a tool that measures opinion—essentially the outcome of what you've done. Opinion research is by far the oldest and most widely used form of measurement. In PR, pre and post surveys are commonly used to determine if a particular program changed opinions or awareness. An initial study establishes a baseline, and a follow-up study determines if opinion has shifted. See Table 3, page 31.

Surveys can be conducted by email, mail, or phone. Typically, results from a mail survey take 4 to 8 weeks. Phone surveys are faster, but can cost 30 to 50 percent more than surveys by mail. Online surveys are rapidly becoming the methodology of choice because they are cheap and relatively easy to field. However, they are only valid if all of your publics have access to a computer and an email account. For a complete list of survey research options,

Survey Tools Compared

Tool	Strengths	Limitations
Online Survey	- easy to program - fast - inexpensive - self-selecting audience	- most are English only - convenience sample (only those who have email addresses)
Paper Survey	- slow - more time to code and analyze - self-selecting audience	- better sampling (reaches everyone)
Phone Survey	- high response rates - fast	- more expensive

Table 3. Comparison of survey tools. Choose the survey tools that best fit your program.

refer to Dr. Don Stacks' *Primer of Public Relations Research* (see Appendix 2).

The Grunig Relationship Survey is the one tool covered in this book that was developed from research that studied the nature of relationships, and was designed specifically to measure relationships and the components of relationships. We cover this survey in detail in Appendix 1. Most of the other tools discussed in this book are commonly used to measure the effectiveness of public relations programs. Although they were not developed specifically to examine relationships, they can provide valuable information and insight.

A serious drawback for surveys can be the time they take to conduct. While I was at Lotus we conducted an annual image study, which was, initially, how we measured our PR results. But we were part of an industry in which the PR picture changed monthly, and I just couldn't wait for a once-a-year study to plan my next move. At the same time I couldn't afford to do our usual form of measurement any more often. So I developed an affordable media analysis system to provide feedback on my program on a monthly or quarterly basis.

Measuring Awareness

Key to measuring PR's involvement in any change in awareness is the ability to isolate the PR activities from any other communications efforts. So PR's effectiveness needs to be tested before any advertising blitz begins. If you are introducing a new product or concept to a marketplace, one that has never been seen or discussed before, it is reasonable to assume that prior to your activity awareness was at zero. If you already have some presence in the marketplace you will need to establish a baseline measurement against which to measure any change in awareness.

Alternately, if advertising and other communications efforts can be maintained at a constant level for a given time (typically 26 weeks), and a PR program is implemented or changed, then the impact of that program can be charted against the steady baseline already established.

Awareness can only be determined by surveying members of the audience at which the PR program is directed. Best practices for this type of research are covered in the Advertising Research Foundation document *Guidelines for Market Research*. See Appendix 2 for more references.

Measuring Preference

"Preference" implies that an individual is making a choice. Therefore, all preference measurements must include alternatives—products or companies that are competitive or that are perceived as being competitive. To determine the impact of public relations outputs on audience preference, you need to expose the audience to the specific output (article, white paper, speech, etc.) and determine whether the piece leaves the audience more or less likely to do business with the company. This exposure can be done in focus groups, panels, or with a randomly selected sample of the population. This last method will generate the highest level of statistical accuracy, but unfortunately is the most expensive of the three.

Measuring Messages: Media Content Analysis

If your objective is exposure and communication of key messages, measuring media content is by far the cheapest, easiest, and fastest form of measurement. In the past, people believed output measurement was simply counting numbers of clips or column inches of media content. But measuring output encompasses far more than calculating sheer volume. It includes looking at the content of each article to determine whether it contains your key messages, how the article leaves the reader feeling, and what messages it communicates. In other words, you need to measure the quality of your PR output as well as the quantity.

To understand this, consider the following example. Which do you think demonstrates a more successful program: A fat notebook containing 500 articles, or a skinny little folder containing 75 articles? The answer, of course, is neither; without examining the content, you have no way of knowing. The former might represent a surge in negative references about the company. The latter might represent a program in which the client communicated its key messages in a whopping 75 percent of the articles, and reached all of its target audiences and 95 percent of its key publications.

In an ideal world, you would poll your entire audience to see what they read and how they react. A more realistic alternative involves having a representative of your target audience read the press clippings and rate them on content and other aspects of coverage. This technique is called media content analysis, and is one of the most valuable and commonly used tools in PR measurement. (Several excellent books on the subject are listed in Appendix 2.) Media content analysis can be done with human readers or can

Media Content Analysis: Manual or Automated?

Tool	Strengths	Limitations
automated content analysis	- can analyze large volumes of articles very quickly to determine share of discussion, share of visibility and share of positioning - very fast - very efficient	- doesn't pull out influencers and spokespeople well - doesn't determine tone - can't determine subtle or complex messages - many foreign publications are not available
manual content analysis	excellent for pulling out complex messaging, tonality and subtle differences	- usually slow, cumbersome - readers can be biased or inconsistent

Table 4. Comparison of manual and automated media content analysis.

be automated (see Table 4, above). During media content analysis, articles are rated on one or more of the following criteria:

Influence or tone—The feeling a reader gets after reading the article; whether or not it leaves a reader more inclined to buy the product or do business with the company.

Messages communicated—Press coverage conveys a variety of messages; some are desirable, some are not. You will want to track key messages established by the company and perhaps others, the good ones as well as the bad. By doing so you may pick up on an early trend that you can leverage to your advantage later. It is often desirable to determine message strength: How strongly are those messages communicated on a scale of one to five?

Prominence—This refers to where in an article the company name appeared, and is used most commonly for competitive analyses. If you are a well-known company like Apple Computer, your name makes headlines, and any story probably will have the company name prominently featured. If you are a smaller company, however, getting your name in a headline can be a rare but important event. A useful classification is:

- Headline–Company/product name is mentioned in a headline.

- Illustration–Company/product name is mentioned in photograph or caption.

- Top 20 percent–Company/product name is mentioned in the top twenty percent of the article.

- Bottom 80 percent–Company/product name is mentioned in the bottom eighty percent of the article.

Dominance—The frequency with which your organization or brand is mentioned in the article. Typically, we rate dominance as:

- Exclusive–Only the company or brand studied is included in the article.

- Dominant

- Average

- Minor

Audience reached—Who saw the article? You can communicate all the messages in the world, but if they never reach your target audience, you've wasted your time. So note the primary audience and/or the media outlet.

Sources mentioned—Influencing the influencers is key for almost all successful programs. So you will want to know if financial analysts, industry gurus, vital customers, user groups, and so forth are picking up your key messages. Who is quoted in your coverage and what do they say?

Article type—Includes product blurbs, industry overviews, reviews, product introductions, application articles, bylines, opinion pieces, and so forth.

Mentions vs. placements—Two frequently confused terms. A placement is synonymous with the appearance of an article. A mention occurs when a given company's name appears in an article. One placement can contain multiple mentions of a given company.

Measuring Outcomes and Behavior

The ultimate test of the effectiveness of your communications efforts is whether the behavior of the target audience has changed as a result. This is also the most difficult to measure because of the other communications and communications efforts that the typical company undertakes. The most effective way to measure behavior change attributable solely to your efforts is to study specific programs carried out by your team, for example, a PR program designed to increase traffic to a restaurant or a museum, or a fundraising effort.

Instant access to Internet data has offered the communications professional a tremendous advantage. Most websites already use some form of traffic analysis such as WebTrends (www.webtrends.com). These systems can tell you very specifically how many people go to what pages on your site. So if you provide a specific URL for a specific press release, you can track editors' and consumers' behavior by following the traffic to that URL. In fact, by tracking visitors' behavior and purchase patterns from its unique URLs, Southwest Airlines has been able to attribute over $5 million in ticket sales to PR. For more information, read the paper at http://www.instituteforpr.com/pdf/Southwest_Airlines_measurement_case.pdf.

Some trade publications offer valuable lead-generation tools in the form of response cards keyed to specific articles. Such leads can frequently be tracked through to sales. However, it must be remembered that although PR generated the lead, the actual sale was heavily influenced by many other factors, such as the distribution channel, availability, and price.

What's It Going to Cost?

The good news is that the rapid advance of technology has driven down the cost of doing measurement, especially data collection and analysis. In fact, there are many tools now available for little or no cost, particularly web-based survey tools. The less obvious bad news result of this is that it is easier than ever to implement a poorly planned study and end up with useless data. It is more important than ever to plan carefully on just what information you want, and what you are going to use it for. Review carefully the Seven Steps in Chapter 1, especially Steps 1 through 4.

The rule of thumb is that you should allocate 10 percent of your overall communications budget for measurement; half for up-front research, the other half for evaluation. The primary driver of expense is the amount of data you collect. The more people you interview, postings you study, or articles you analyze, the higher the cost.

There are many estimates of cost for both surveys and media analysis, but they change with each advance of technology. Your best estimating strategy is to prepare a detailed RFP (Request for Proposal) and submit it to a variety of vendors (see the list of resources at www.measuresofsuccess.com).

Cost Factors for Surveys

If you are going to survey an audience, here's what influences the cost:

Number of questionnaires administered—You can probably get most of the information you need from talking to 250 people. If you are skeptical, note that it's possible to get a representative sample of the entire United States with only 500 people.

So don't get talked into surveying thousands if you don't really need to.

Length of questionnaire—It's always a good idea to keep your questionnaire as short as possible, as it holds down the cost, and it brings up your level of response. A quantitative survey should take no more than ten minutes to administer.

Cost of collecting names—For example, if you are studying an event, you would collect names and phone numbers only and interview by phone after the event. That way you know what they remember about you, not just what their initial impression was.

Difficulty in getting people to respond—You may need to offer incentives to get people to respond, or repeatedly ask them to respond. Marketers, for instance, are notoriously difficult to survey; even journalists and doctors are easier. You also need to make sure that every member has an equal opportunity to participate. The more random your selection, the better. Self-selecting groups (e.g., people who come to your website) are much less desirable, because those people interested in the topic are more likely to participate, thus skewing your results. What you may really need are the opinions of people who are *not* going to your website.

Customized vs. syndicated research—On any given day there are thousands of research projects going on that research firms and publications hope to sell to every company in a particular industry. Contact the leading research firms and/or industry trade publications to find out if there's a project that applies to you. Another option is to add questions to omnibus studies that regularly survey the population at large. The typical price is $3,000 for one or two questions.

Cost Factors for Media Content Analysis

Commercial clipping organizations charge between $1 and $3 a clip to gather articles, and analysis firms can charge upwards of $30 per article to analyze the content. You can expect these costs to come down as technology makes this work faster and easier. Other cost influences are:

How many media outlets are you analyzing? Eighty percent of your most meaningful and effective articles will come from twenty percent of your publications. Therefore, the easiest way to cut down on volume is to limit your search to the twenty percent that really matter.

Are you collecting everything, or just those stories that have the greatest likelihood of being seen? Many articles, even in your top-gun publications, will be not relevant to your study. Such articles would include coverage of weddings, minor promotions, and company events. Discard these articles.

If you're still faced with more articles than you know what to do with, limit your selection to those articles that mention you in the headline or lead paragraph, because that's all the average reader pays attention to anyway. These articles are the ones that are going to have the biggest impact in the long run.

If You Have No Budget at All

Be someone's homework. My company, KDPaine & Partners, was previously located in Durham, New Hampshire. We were blessed by the proximity of the University of New Hampshire, which has an excellent market research lab. Most MBA programs and undergraduate colleges offer some sort of survey research class. With a bit of luck and persuasion, you can get them to conduct the research for you.

Start with baby steps. An annual measurement program can be a sizeable undertaking, and if your organization hasn't done one before it is a daunting process. I highly recommend beginning with a pilot program, either a three-month benchmark or a targeted program aimed at a particular launch or event. This relatively painless route will get people addicted to the numbers, and they'll invariably ask for more.

Finally, if you encounter resistance from management for the funding of your measurement program, ask them these two questions: How much money do we spend talking to our clients? Can't we talk better if we spend some time listening? Listening is what communications measurement and PR research is all about.

Chapter 3

Measuring Relationships with the Media

Communication is not what you send out, but what arrives.
—Jim Macnamara

Traditionally, organizations have measured their media relations in one of three ways: outputs, outtakes, and outcomes (see the Glossary for more detailed definitions). Output measures examine the physical production of your PR program. Outtake measures examine what the reporter has personally taken away as a result of your efforts. Both are perfectly valid, and we'll discuss them in more detail under Step 5, later in this chapter.

I believe, however, that the most important measures of your media relations efforts are the outcomes that you generate in the media itself. If you want to measure your relationship with the media, then looking at their behavior—i.e., what they are writing about you—is much more important than knowing what they think about you personally. That's not to say that you shouldn't occasionally survey reporters and editors to better understand your relationship, but it wouldn't be the first measure I'd suggest.

Given that it is the media's job to report on what it considers news, the best you can hope for as an outcome is that the media covers you fairly and accurately on a regular basis. That is, ultimately, the desired outcome of your program. To measure that

**Typical Outputs, Outtakes, and Outcomes
for Measuring the Media**

Outputs: Percentage pick up in key media of news from press releases; percentage of articles containing key messages; share of visibility relative to the competition; share of positive and negative coverage relative to the competition

Outtakes: Percentage change in awareness of new initiatives; percentage change in perception of your position on key battles or issues

Outcomes: Percentage change in website traffic; percentage change in requests for information; percentage change in market share, sales, attendance, or donations

outcome you need to closely analyze the content of your press coverage to determine the extent to which reporters are writing about your organization in an accurate and balanced way, positioning you vis-a-vis the competition in ways that are beneficial to your organization, using your messages, and relying on the sources you provide for information. This process is called media content analysis, and is one of the most valuable measurement tools at your disposal. For a more detailed discussion, see Chapter 2, Tools and Costs.

The following procedure for measuring your relationship with the media follows the general framework of the Seven Steps laid out in Chapter 1, and largely involves media content analysis. Refer back to that chapter for more details about each step, but keep in mind that, because every audience is different, not every step in this chapter will be exactly like that in Chapter 1.

Seven Steps to Measure Your Relationship with the Media

Step 1: Determine and Prioritize Your Audience

In this case your audience is the media. If your relationship with the media is healthy, then coverage will accurately reflect your positioning on issues that are important to you. So the first thing to do is to determine what subset of the media is most relevant to your organization and issues. You may very well have to work on Step 2 below at the same time as this one, because the importance of certain issues may help to determine which media are of interest.

As anyone who has dealt with TV news crews knows, there is no such thing as "the media." Television reporters have vastly different requirements than print journalists, who have different needs than radio or online journalists, who are different still from financial reporters, lifestyle editors, and so on. So segment your media into categories relevant to your organization and your issues (see Table 5, page 44 for examples).

It's not cheap to gather clips or analyze articles, so unless you have an unlimited budget, you will need to prioritize the media to determine just which media outlets and what articles you are going to analyze.

Priorities should always be set based on the ultimate benefit to your organization. Here's an example. One of my clients was an electronic game manufacturer. While coverage in the local press may have been good for the boss' ego, the business ultimately depended on getting information about new games to their primary target audience, teenage boys. So for the media list for this client, we included a few key business books and virtually all of the gaming and lifestyle publications. By the way, an important point here, as in most media analysis, is that the people we had analyze the articles were members of the target audience. Most electronic game publications are incomprehensible to your average adult, so we hired teenagers to clip and analyze the publications.

You may want to prioritize the media you will be analyzing by who reads them. Almost all publications list their circulations with the Audit Bureau of Circulations (www.accessabc.com) and Standard Rate & Data (www.srds.com). Depending on the target audience that your organization wants to reach, you can use those sources to select only the most appropriate media

■ Print	■ Lifestyle
■ TV	■ Sports
■ Radio	■ Business to business
■ Online 'zines	■ Vertical market
■ Blogs	■ Hispanic
■ Local weeklies	■ Educational
■ Local dailies	■ Circulation under 50,000
■ Local TV	■ Circulation 50K–100K
■ Financial	■ Circulation 100K and above
■ Business	■ YouTube or other CGM

Table 5. Media categories to consider for analysis.

outlets to track, based on the circulation and demographic data for the publications.

Step 2: Determine the Issues

You must determine which issues are most important to your organization and/or program, because only then can you move on to selecting specific criteria in Step 3. Also, the importance of certain issues may help determine the importance of certain media, so you may have to work on this step concurrently with Step 1 above. Some examples of general issues that might be most important to your organization are listed in Table 6, page 45.

Step 3: Define Specific Criteria of Success

The next step in the process is to define the specific criteria by which you will determine the success of your program. In other words: What can you measure that will give you a number that

- ■ Investment of choice
- ■ Financially sound
- ■ Well managed / good management team
- ■ Honest / ethical
- ■ Socially responsible
- ■ Environmentally responsible
- ■ Delivers on time
- ■ High quality service

- ■ High quality goods
- ■ Employer of choice
- ■ Great place to work
- ■ Great place for women to work
- ■ Partner of choice
- ■ Good value for the money
- ■ Responsive

Table 6. Commonly tracked issues.

will indicate whether or not your PR program is working? See Figure 4, page 46 for some sample charts showing criteria of success for a competitive media analysis. The most typical criteria include:

- ■ **Share of opportunities to see**—Of all the opportunities to see a brand or product in your market, how much is of your product or brand compared to that of the competition?

- ■ **Share of visibility**—Of all the highly visible coverage (coverage that includes your brand or product in the headline, a caption, a photo or in the first paragraph of a story), how much is about your product or brand compared to that of the competition?

- ■ **Share of recommendations**—Of all the times editors or analysts recommend a brand or product, how often is your brand or product mentioned versus the competition? While most reporters don't editorialize on specific products, there are certainly times, especially in product

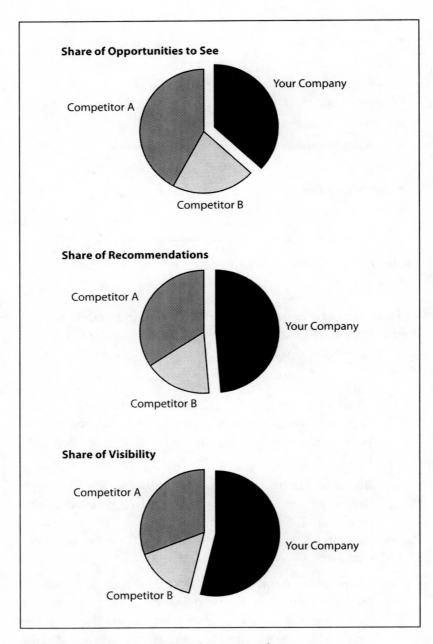

Figure 4. Charts of typical criteria of success.

reviews, where they recommend one product or service over another. You want to make sure that of all the times that happens, you are mentioned as often if not more than the competition.

- **Share of analysts' quotes**—Of all the times key industry analysts are quoted, how often do they mention your brand or product compared to that of the competition?

- **Share of spokespeople quoted**—Of all the times company spokespeople are mentioned, how often are they from your company versus the competition?

- **Share of brand benefit mentions**—Of all the times coverage mentions brand benefits, how often is your brand mentioned?

- **Share of positioning**—Organizations frequently aim to position themselves as leaders, innovators, or best places to work. Such positioning requires a clear understanding of the issues (see Step 2 above) that drive customers to buy your product, donate, join, or whatever else it is that you are trying to get your constituencies to do. What you need to do is determine what positioning is most effective at persuading customers. You then need to track all the times articles mention such positioning, and note how many mention your brand versus the competition.

- **Share of negative versus positive reviews**—You also want to make sure that you minimize any negative references, particularly in product reviews. Some negative press is inevitable—someone or some product always has to come in last in a review—but you want to make sure that of all the negatives that appear, your share is minimal.

- **Share of dominant coverage**—When you are analyzing your media coverage it is important to note how and where in the story your organization is mentioned, since such placement will impact the degree to which people will remember seeing your news. If you are the major focus of a story your presence in that story is much more likely to register than if you are simply a passing reference. The key to success therefore is to get the greatest share of dominant coverage and minimize your share of peripheral mentions.

■ **Percentage of articles containing key messages**—Key messages are those specific statements or concepts that you are trying to communicate to your various publics. A key message is unique to your organization (or at least it should be) and it must be something that a journalist is likely to print. It is therefore critical to track both the quantity and content of the messages in your media coverage. Typically you should look at the entire body of mentions and determine what percentage contains at least one message. You should also look to see how much exposure you are getting for each message. This will help you determine which messages need reinforcing either by paid advertising, or by increased emphasis on the part of key spokespeople.

■ **Percentage increase in traffic month-to-month to specific PR areas on your website**— If your media relations is designed to encourage audiences to go to your website, create a specific URL for each press release so you can determine the extent to which that release is responded to. If you mention or are promoting specific references or white papers, post them with unique URLs to see which are being viewed or downloaded.

■ **Percentage increase in media registrations each month**— If you have a press room on your website where journalists can register to receive more information, track those registrations each month and measure the percent increase over previous months.

Step 4: Decide on a Benchmark

Measurement is by its nature a comparative tool, so determine what you will be evaluating your results against. The best option is key competitors or perceived competitors. Peer organizations can also be useful. The least desirable option is to simply look at your own results over time, because you don't know whether your results reflect success or failure until you compare them to what other companies are achieving.

Step 5: Select Your Measurement Tool

The selection of the right tool for your specific organization depends entirely on the criteria with which you defined success in Step 3 above. Those criteria all require some form of media content analysis to determine your results. However, there are other tools available that you may want to consider. See Chapter 2 for more on measurement tools.

Clips, cuttings, articles, transcripts—whatever you want to call them—represent your best measurement of what the media currently thinks about you and how the influencers in your particular market perceive you. However, how you collect the clips is crucial to the validity of your study. If you are using a clipping service, you probably are working within a universe of publications defined by you or the service. If you are studying your competition, you also must gather their articles from the same universe.

A Word About Coding Articles

Remember that communications professionals do not read the media like normal human beings: We are far too quick to spot a key message (particularly our own) and are much more sensitive to reporters' opinions. Ideally you should find a member of your target audience to analyze the media. If you're selling networks, get a network manager to evaluate it. If you're selling video games, find a teenager. Or, if your volume of coverage justifies it, you can use one of half a dozen automated content analysis programs such as those from Cymfony (www.cymfony.com) or Biz360 (www.biz360.com).

Tools to Measure Media Outtakes: The Journalist Audit

While outcomes are the most important measure of success of a media relations program, outtakes and outputs have their value as well. Outtake measures reflect how journalists think and feel about your organization. By periodically checking in with them, you can gain valuable insight as to why your programs are performing as they do.

Keeping in touch with journalists is very important. When I was at Lotus, we discovered that one reviewer in particular was likely to be negative toward our products. As it turned out, we had shipped him a product to review that didn't work. Worse still, we hadn't followed up, and he had called several times for help and not been satisfied with the responses we provided. We were eventually able to turn his negatives into positives by solving his problems, but we wouldn't have been able to do that had we not asked him about our relationship.

There are a number of ways you can solicit the opinions of journalists, but *do not* simply call up your media contacts and ask them questions. Use an independent third party to ensure that the answers aren't biased. You also should make sure you use questions that will get the desired results. The Grunig Relationship Survey is a series of agree/disagree statements that are excellent tests of a relationship and I use them frequently on reporters. The reporter is presented with a list of statements and asked whether he or she agrees or disagrees with the statements on a 1-7 or 1-9 scale. Typical statements that you might want to include in a journalist audit include (a complete list of the Grunig questions is in Appendix 1):

How to Set Up Your Own Simple Tracking System

Once you've collected your articles, arrange a simple numbering system to keep track of them. For example, in an analysis by quarter you might want to start with 1000 for the first quarter, 2000 for the second quarter, and so on. Number each article and record the basic details:

- Date of appearance
- Publication
- Reporter
- Type of article
- Person quoted

These facts can be written down by anyone. If you're getting clips from a service that provides the circulation of the publication, record the circulation figure as well.

- This organization treats me fairly and justly.
- This organization can be relied on to keep its promises.
- This organization has the ability to accomplish what it says it will do.
- I can see that this organization wants to maintain a relationship with me.

Another option is to hire a vendor to do the work. GfK (www.gfk.com), ASQ (www.asq.org) and other major research firms periodically conduct journalist audits, and, for a fee, they'll include your company. This is a particularly good way of getting information out of journalists, since they are notoriously hard to reach. However, if you do not have a major brand name that will register strongly with journalists, you may not have very useful results.

Tools to Measure the Outputs of Your Media Relations Program

Establish simple process measures for your PR department to understand how well it is functioning. These measures can be as simple as looking at how efficient the department is at responding to requests for information or at writing press releases. Criteria such as "response time to department requests," or "number of incoming journalist requests handled" may seem highly simplistic, but they can yield useful information in terms of staffing and planning needs.

Cost per impression, or more specifically cost per thousand impressions (CPM), is a universal criterion that is used by advertisers in print, broadcast, and online. It is based on the total reach of your efforts; in other words, how many eyeballs you reached and at what cost. To calculate CPM you take your budget for the month or quarter, and divide it by the number of opportunities to see (OTS, also known as impressions) that you generated during the same time frame.

My favorite criterion among output measures is to look at the cost per message communicated. Just how much does it cost you to get a message in front of your target audience? This number is calculated by dividing the budget for the quarter by the total number of opportunities to see (OTS) the messages (see Figure 5, page 53). To get the OTS for each message, add up the total circulation of the publications in which articles containing key messages have appeared. If more than one article has appeared in a particular publication, then count that publication's circulation once for each article that appeared.

Reviewed over a period of time, such data can tell you clearly what size staff is necessary to achieve a desired outcome. When we measured Apple Computer's results I noticed that its coverage doubled in May and continued at that level for the rest of the year. As it turned out, it had doubled its staff in February. The lesson here is that if you want to achieve a certain level of coverage, you'll need the staff to do it. Measuring your department's outputs is the way to understand how much staff it requires.

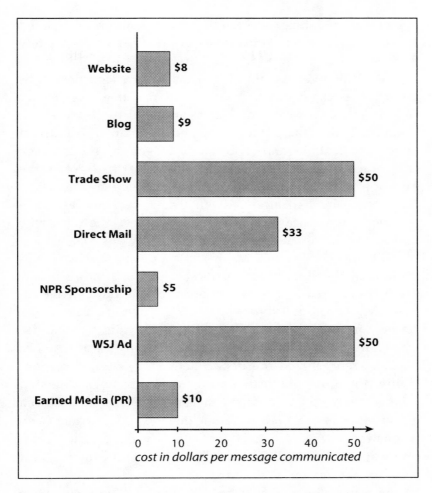

Figure 5. Using cost per message communicated to compare the effectiveness of different tactics. How much does it cost to get your message in front of your target audience?

Message analysis can also be used to improve staff performance. Once, when I was director of corporate communications for a large software company, we had just completed a major product launch. Unfortunately, a significant percentage of articles written about the new product failed to communicate our key messages and in fact completely mispositioned the product. My first impulse was to question the effectiveness of using a major press party for the launch, because over the years I'd learned that free shrimp seldom makes for clear message communication. However, upon analyzing the launch coverage in detail to figure out which publications and reporters had "gotten" the message and which had not, and whether those that had gotten the message were at our event, the data proved inconclusive. Reporters who had attended our event were just as likely to have communicated our key messages as the ones who had stayed home and read the press kit.

But another interesting statistic popped out as I was reviewing the data: Almost all the mispositioning of the product occurred in a certain segment of the trade media—in this case, those publications specifically covering large mainframe computer issues. Now what made this particularly interesting to me as the department manager was that we had just reorganized the department and assigned responsibility for those publications to a young but very talented PR manager. Just to confirm my suspicions, I interviewed a few reporters to find out what their experience had been in dealing with my department—hardly the formal "communications audit" I'd normally recommend, but the best tool I could muster at the time.

As it turned out, they'd had difficulty getting their phone calls returned. Surprised, I took my concerns to the offending manager, only to find out that she resented her new assignment, believing that it was less prestigious than her old one and that she had been effectively demoted. She had vented her frustration by spending time planning her wedding rather than returning phone calls. After I explained that this particular group of editors was vital to the company's future, and accurate messaging in this audience was a key measure of her success, her behavior quickly changed.

Other output measures might include:

- **Percentage of coverage reaching the target audience**—Of all the opportunities to see your messages or information, how much reached the right audience and/or appeared in your top-tier publications?

- **Department share of leadership**—What percentage of projects does your department participate in versus what percentage of your department members have a leadership role?

- **Networking**—To what extent are you included in industry or community groups?

- **Credibility**—To what extent is your staff or department sought out for its expertise?

- **Accuracy**—What percentage of overall coverage is accurate in terms of product specifications, descriptions, names, and so forth?

- **Efficiency**—What percentage of your press release distribution list actually covers you on a regular basis? What percentage of the reporter contacts are still at the publications and what percentage of them are actively writing about your industry?

Accounting for the Reach of Wire Stories

For some reason, accounting for the reach of wire stories has always sparked a spirited debate. Wire stories fall into two categories. The first are stories you pay to put up on Business Wire, PR Newswire, or other paid distribution services. These should not be included in your media analysis since they haven't been picked up by anyone and actually published.

The second type of wire stories are those that make it onto the Associated Press, Reuters, or UPI wires. If a story appears on one of these wires, an editor in one of these organizations has

---

A Word about Circulation Figures

You will frequently hear the term "impression" or "opportunity to see" mentioned in the context of media analysis. Impressions are defined as the total audited circulation of a publication. Readership, credibility, and significance vary tremendously between publications, between geographic locations, and between industries. Since no statistically valid data exist across the nation to indicate when an article is more credible, or more widely read in one location than another, we do not recommend placing any artificial multiples on the audited circulation figures.

---

decided that your story is newsworthy enough to send it out to its subscribers. However, that doesn't mean that anyone has seen it other than the editor and the people at the subscribing organizations who check the wire feed. Once again, the story hasn't yet been picked up by anyone and actually published. This is why we assign a circulation figure of 1 to all wire stories.

If your story gets picked up by an actual publication or media outlet, then the circulation of that media outlet should be included in the media analysis. If the story does not get picked up, and only appears on one or more of the wires, it means that none of the subscribing outlets thought your story was newsworthy. Their circulation figures should not be included in the analysis.

Step 6: Compare Results to Objectives and Draw Actionable Conclusions

Once you've collected and analyzed your data, you need to translate the results into appropriate charts and graphs. As with all your data analyses, make sure your analysis is pursuing and illustrating actionable results—results that apply to relevant programs that you can do something about and that your company bosses *want* to do something about. Don't measure dead products or competitors that aren't viable or publications you

Data Persuasion

Have you ever had a hard time persuading an executive to go on a press tour? Show them a chart indicating the potential disaster if they don't go. Once when a client was preparing for a press tour, I pointed out that all the publications on the itinerary were questioning the company's financial viability. When I asked who was going out on the tour, they said the product developer. I questioned whether he would be able to answer questions about the financial issues (and obviously, he wouldn't). But I was told that the general manager "doesn't do press tours." I suggested that this manager be shown a chart of the publications' interests. Not only was he convinced to go along on the tour, but his presence on it diffused skepticism over the company's financial viability. None of the subsequent articles contained negative financial messages.

don't have time to target. Most importantly, you need to put the data to work in ways that will encourage decisions that will yield tangible results.

Step 7: Take Action and Measure Again

When measuring your relationships with the media, it is important to remember how quickly and often the media can change. That's why you need to look at data on a regular basis—at least once a quarter, if not once a month—to see the impact of any changes you've made. Set up a regular reporting timetable. This helps in meetings, but it also ensures that you have the data in hand when you're making decisions. Plan on having the right data at your fingertips as you start your planning or budgeting process. Collecting data at the end of the year is fine, but make sure that the analysis and conclusions are ready when you need to make important decisions.

Chapter 4

Measuring Relationships with Analysts and Influencers

Facts do not cease to exist because they are ignored.
—Aldous Huxley

A good communications program functions like a food chain. You educate key spokespeople and influencers on your message, and, assuming it's the right message, it flows down through the chain of media and ultimately reaches your publics through a variety of credible sources.

The most critical elements in many communications programs are the spokespeople and influencers. This group is made up of thought leaders, early adopters, industry analysts, financial analysts, key customers, academics, leadership figures, and just about any person that others turn to for advice and recommendations. In cosmetics, it is hair stylists. In high tech, it is the key industry consultants. In automobiles, it is the car enthusiasts. Every industry has them, and every marketer targets them with varying degrees of success.

Do They Recommend Your Product?

As with journalists, the ultimate measure of a successful relationship with analysts and influencers is if they recommend your product to reporters, editors, and customers. The methodology

---

**Typical Outputs, Outtakes, and Outcomes
for Measuring Analysts and Influencers**

Outputs: Number of analysts attending press events; number of analysts writing about you

Outtakes: Percent change in analysts understanding and/or believing your key messages

Outcomes: Change in number of recommendations/quotes by analysts/influencers; change in public perceptions; increase in desired behaviors among your constituencies

---

for measuring your results is similar to that for the media. You first collect articles, transcripts, and mentions in publications that your customers are reading. Then you analyze those publications to determine which sources their editors and reporters turn to for advice and information. Ultimately you should interview those sources to find out what they are really thinking about your product or your position in the industry.

Here's an example. The beauty care division of a major consumer packaged goods company was trying to figure out how to improve its overall awareness and preference with its target customers—women between the ages of 18 and 35. It knew that this audience read the top fifteen beauty books for advice, but it wasn't sure how to influence those publications. My firm conducted a "share of ink" study to determine how much coverage each of their product categories—hair care, facial care, sun screen, etc.—received during the course of the year. We looked at all the articles about those products and quickly established that hair stylists and salon owners were most frequently quoted.

So our client then made an effort to reach out to those groups, both in industry-specific trade publications and with events and specially tailored programs. Ultimately, the media analysis effort yielded a rich database that allowed our client to spot trends in product recommendations, and tie those to promotional efforts. It could also establish its firm's share of recommendations against other firms in the industry. Their final, ideal result is to tie the firm's share of recommendations to market share data.

To get started with your own measurement program, determine which influencers are important and to what extent you are top-of-mind with them. Use a database, spreadsheet, or analysis module to record—for every article about you, your industry, or your competition—the name of the publication, the name of the reporter and of everyone quoted. This will give you a list of most frequently quoted sources. Also record several other details about each article: Was it entirely about you or your industry or category? Did the influencer quoted refer directly to your organization, or was the quote about someone else? And finally, did the article and/or quote contain one or more of your key messages?

The next step is to gain a better understanding of how the influencers feel about you and your organization. I recommend regular annual relationship surveys, conducted by phone or email. Ask about the extent to which they understand your strategies and mission, the extent to which they believe in your management's ability, and their overall image of—and trust in—your organization. You can use many of the same techniques that you use in journalist audits, asking questions based on the Grunig Relationship Survey (see Appendix 1), such as:

- This organization has the ability to accomplish what it says it will do.

- In dealing with people like me, this organization has a tendency to throw its weight around.

- I would rather work together with this organization than not.

- Most people enjoy dealing with this organization.

Special Considerations for Tracking Analysts

With opinion leaders it is particularly important to compare your organization to your peers and competitors, since they will no doubt be pitching competing messages and stories to the same opinion leaders. Be sure to ask them how your organization ranks in their minds relative to others in the industry.

One factor that you need to consider when evaluating opinion-leader relations is the impact of consultant/client relationships. Frequently, industry analysts and opinion leaders are paid consultants to one or more organizations. Their access to inside knowledge of an organization is why they are considered opinion leaders and is an important part of the work they are paid to do. What this means, however, is that your status or lack thereof as a client has a direct effect on their opinions. It is worth noting in your database whether they are a consultant to your organization, or to one of your competitors.

It is also important to integrate your research with other events within your organization. Here's an example: Tracy Eiler, formerly at Business Objects, had been tracking analyst relations for a number of years. When budgets got tight a few years ago, she was forced to eliminate a position that was specifically charged with maintaining analyst relations. The following reporting period saw a dramatic decline in how the analyst community viewed Business Objects, particularly on the subject of responsiveness. Without the extra person, the company just couldn't be as responsive as it had been in the past. She charted the drop and subsequent decline in quotes in the media, presented the results to her boss, and the position was re-established.

Tracking analysts can also help identify new opportunities for influence. At one time a few years ago, we were tracking a core list of critical analysts that a major computer company had established. As it turned out, some of the members of that list were seldom quoted, and from time to time there were quotes from new names. By providing our client with a update of active influencers each month, we were able to continuously improve the effectiveness of the analyst relations effort.

Case Study: The New Hampshire Political Library

Tracking influencers and carefully tailoring your messages to them can have a major impact on one's reputation. One study of New Hampshire's reputation in the media revealed that it appeared to be populated by flannel-shirted hicks, citizens that didn't deserve their unusual political influence as voters in the first-in-the-nation presidential primary.

A group of state leaders headed by former governor Hugh Gregg decided they needed to change this perception. The New Hampshire Political Library (NHPL), which Gregg founded, conducted a detailed media analysis of New Hampshire's presidential primary coverage. After reading and analyzing some 3,000 articles that referred to the state of New Hampshire's attributes and failings, they had a list of the reporters and journalists who were most likely to visit or write about the state. Additionally, they were able to isolate two dozen influencers who journalists regularly went to for information about the state or the primary. They then provided those influencers with facts and figures about the state, such as:

- New Hampshire has the highest per capita number of high-tech jobs in the country.

- There are over two hundred languages spoken in the Manchester school system.

- New Hampshire citizens participate in politics in greater frequency than citizens of any other state in the union: 75 percent have voted in the primary, 74 percent have

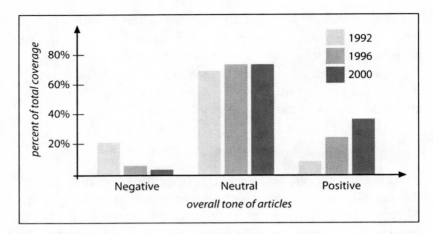

Figure 6. Graph of the dramatic change in tone of New Hampshire's coverage from 1992 to 2000. The graph illustrates how improving relationships with influencers can positively affect coverage.

watched a debate or have otherwise paid attention, and 13 percent have attended an event.

■ One in ten New Hampshire residents have shaken the hand of a candidate.

The NHPL also worked with the leaders of both political parties (who were on the list of top influencers) to change candidates' photo-op venues. Prior to the 2000 election year, most presidential candidates' photos had been staged around maple trees and in diners. As a result of the efforts of NHPL, most of the photo-ops in 2000 occurred in high-tech factories and manufacturing venues.

The result of all these efforts was that the overall tone of coverage dramatically shifted (see Figure 6, above). Journalists who once had described New Hampshire citizens as "backwards," "quirky," or "persnickety" were now saying that the state deserved the primary because of its citizens' intense level of political engagement (see Figure 7, page 65, and Figure 8,

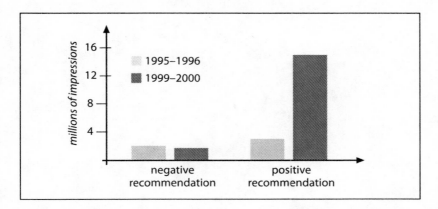

Figure 7. Endorsement of New Hampshire as a desirable place increases, 1995 to 2000.

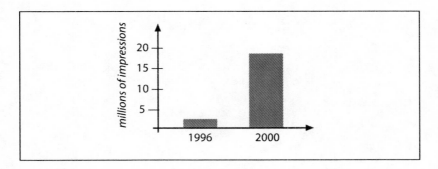

Figure 8. "First in the Nation" key message is communicated more frequently in 2000 than 1996.

above). Further analysis showed that the messages were frequently communicated in quotations from influencers identified in the earlier study (see R. Gittell and B. Gottlob, "The Economic Impact of New Hampshire's First-in-the-Nation Primary," Library and Archives of New Hampshire's Political Tradition, February 2001).

Chapter 5

Comparing Media Relations to Other Marketing Disciplines

He uses statistics as a drunken man uses lamp-posts . . .
for support rather than illumination.

—Andrew Lang

Sooner or later, someone will probably ask you to compare the effectiveness or value of different marketing disciplines. Given the competition for corporate resources and the ever-increasing demand for results accountability, this is not an unreasonable request. But it is often difficult to comply with, and the temptation to use convenient but invalid methods is great. There are proven, valid approaches to comparing the value of marketing efforts, several of which we will survey in this chapter. But first we must deal with advertising value equivalency (AVE), a common but mostly discredited technique.

The Problems with Advertising Value Equivalency

PR people are often asked for one comparison technique in particular: advertising value equivalency, commonly referred to as AVE. AVEs appear in several slightly different forms, all of which involve applying the dollar cost of an ad space purchase to the amount of earned media coverage achieved by PR efforts. There are a number of problems with AVEs, starting with the fact that public relations and advertising are two different disciplines,

---

**Typical Outputs, Outtakes, and Outcomes for Comparing
Media Relations to Other Marketing Disciplines**

Outputs: Relative number of opportunities to see generated by media relations
versus other marketing/communications tactics; relative cost per opportunity to see
key messages; PR value ratio

Outtakes: Percent awareness or preference generated by PR versus other marketing/
communications tactics

Outcomes: Percent change in sales; percent change in market share generated by
PR versus other tactics

---

designed to do different things in different ways. Comparing the
two with AVEs is the equivalent of hiring a plumber to redo your
bathroom, and then calling in a house painter to get a price quote
to do the same thing. You just can't compare the two jobs.

Secondly, the AVE methodology has no research to support
its validity; there is no scientific evidence to demonstrate that a
six column-inch ad has the same impact as a six-inch story in the
same publication. Ads and articles are different things, and they
affect the reader differently. Ads typically include photographs,
are supposed to include key messages, and are designed to leave
the reader more likely to purchase the product or do business
with the company. On the other hand, only one in five earned
media articles includes a key message, or leaves the reader more
likely to do business with the company. And fewer than 5 percent
include a photograph of the product. Keep in mind that PR is
usually filtered through an editorial or other media source, so
it has comparatively more credibility than straight advertising.
The point here is that to treat earned media and advertising as
somehow equivalent in their impact per square inch is unfounded
and simply incorrect.

In addition, if you apply a standard metric across all articles, you neglect to account for the credibility of the placement or the reputation of the publication, both of which can vary considerably. Some articles appear where advertising can't be bought; take the front page of *The Wall Street Journal*, for example. How would you compare the influence of an ad in the *National Enquirer* to a front-page story in the same publication? The ad appears in the back, and no one reads it. But millions see the front page. Consider how readers experience articles and ads in trade publications. One technical article on a product might take a reader five minutes to peruse and he or she may send the article on to colleagues for future collaboration. That almost never happens with an ad.

And if the problems with AVE's unproven concept weren't enough, many organizations use obviously flawed methodology in their calculations. Commercial services such as Bacons and Burrelle's, who provide AVE figures as part of their measurement reports, calculate their AVEs based on advertising open rates. However, most advertisers purchase ads on an annual contract, or at least contract for multiple insertions, and pay actual ad prices significantly lower than open rates. So while your clipping service may tell you that your PR ad equivalency cost is $100,000, that ad space might typically have been bought for less than $50,000.

On average, 10 to 20 percent of earned media coverage is negative, yet most companies include this coverage in their AVE calculations, even though it would not be the sort of coverage one would want to purchase or would appear in an ad. As an example, one insurance company we worked with was proud of their soaring AVE numbers. Closer examination of their coverage, however, showed that much of it was negative, that their ratio of positive to negative coverage was declining, and that few of their key messages were getting out. Their AVE numbers, which could not take any of these aspects into account, erroneously indicated that their coverage was healthy and improving, when in reality the opposite was the case.

If AVEs are so obviously flawed, why are they so popular? The main reason is that they are quick and easy to calculate, and typically provide a very flattering assessment of PR's value. So when managers insist that they want a fast and cheap dollar figure placed on PR results, AVEs are a tempting and convenient—but essentially meaningless—solution. Worse than meaningless, actually, because those who settle for AVEs often don't make the effort to pursue more valid and useful measurement techniques.

Having given that caveat, however, there have been occasional situations in which AVEs have been found useful. At least one measurement program has found reasonably close correlation between AVEs and sales figures. There have been recent efforts to improve AVEs by leaving out negative coverage and by using ad rates that reflect those actually paid for ads. Still, until there is solid research, validation, and standardization behind their methodology, AVEs will remain unproven and discredited.

How to Measure Your PR Success Against Other Marketing Disciplines

The techniques outlined in the following pages are based on statistics derived from media content analysis. Like AVEs they do not measure customer response or outcomes, outtakes, or behavioral success. But unlike AVEs, they are valid comparisons. Each of these techniques identifies a common measurable effect for PR and another marketing discipline, then compares that measurable effect to contrast the two disciplines. This is a relatively new approach to measurement, and I suspect there are similar but as-yet-undiscovered techniques that would be effective in certain circumstances. Whatever technique you use, make sure your boss buys into it before you invest too much time and energy.

CPM: Cost per Impression or Cost per Thousand Eyeballs Reached

CPM is a standard metric used in advertising (online, print, and broadcast), in sponsorship, trade shows, and many other forms of marketing. It works just as well for media relations. However, one caveat to remember is that CPM is only an expression of reach, not penetration of key messages (we'll deal with key messages in the next section, on cost per message communicated).

To determine CPM for a given time period, first add up the total circulation figures for all the outlets in which a story appeared that mentioned your brand, product, or organization over that time period. We call this number "total opportunities to see" your brand.

Now, divide your total opportunities to see into your PR costs for the same period. Include all your costs (staff and agency), as well as direct expenses. The result is the cost per opportunity for one person to see your brand in earned media. For some reason, advertising folks have decided that they would calculate this figure not based on an individual person, but based on the cost to reach 1,000 people, so you need to multiply the total by 1,000. The result is CPM, and you can compare this figure between marketing vehicles.

Not All Impressions Are Good Impressions

The CPM computation technique is easy to calculate but fairly crude, as it includes any and all impressions. If you have the data available, you will make more accurate comparisons by including in your analysis only those articles that meet certain criteria. For example, we typically categorize articles as to whether or not they include key messages, and whether or not they are positive, negative, or neutral. Positive articles are those that leave a member of your target audience *more* likely to purchase the product or do business with the company. Negative articles are those that leave a member of your target audience *less* likely to purchase the product or do business with the company. Neutral articles are those that leave a member of your target audience neither more nor less likely to purchase the product or do business with the company.

Computing CPM for Press Releases versus Advertising

Suppose you issue a press release that gets picked up in ten outlets with a total combined circulation of 500,000. The agency sends you a bill for $5,000 for producing and distributing the press release. The CPM for the press release is:

($5,000/500,000 impressions) x 1000 = (1/100) x 1000 = $10

Let's say that to buy advertising to get the brand in front of the same 500,000 eyeballs, it would cost $50,000. Then the CPM for advertising would be $100.

So, to make impressions in this hypothetical example, advertising costs ten times more than a press release.

You can use similar calculations to compute CPM for your website or other marketing vehicle. A lower CPM means the vehicle reaches more of your audience (makes more impressions) at a lower cost.

When comparing the effectiveness of different marketing disciplines, you will usually (depending on your specific purposes) achieve more accurate results if you use only those articles that are not negative, or only those articles that include key messages (see the following section, on CPMC). This is not to say you should always ignore unfavorable articles or mentions. You may wish to study them in particular, to learn how you can keep them to a minimum.

CPMC: Cost per Message Communicated

If your department's specific mission is to communicate the company's messages, cost per message communicated (CPMC) is a very good measure of your effectiveness and efficiency. This technique is just like that above for CPM, but is based on the number of message impressions, rather than simple article impressions. For the sake of argument, we can assume that ads always communicate key messages, so the advertising CPM and

Using CPM and CPMC to Compare the Effectiveness of Two Press Events

Suppose you wished to compare a press conference and a press tour as to how effective they were at communicating key messages. Let's assume the press conference cost $25,000 to produce and resulted in ten articles in a variety of trade publications. Let's assume that the press tour cost $50,000 to produce and resulted in ten articles in local daily newspapers plus two mentions on local TV. Here's how to compute cost per opportunity to see for each event.

First, determine which articles included key messages, and then find the circulation of each media outlet in which they appeared. Circulation figures are generally available from your clipping service or Standard Rate and Data Services.

For the press conference, let's assume that five of the ten articles in the trade publications contained a key message, and that the total circulation of those publications is 100,000. Then total opportunities to see a key message equals 5 x 100,000 = 500,000. To determine CPMC, divide the cost of the event by the opportunities to see: $25,000 ÷ 500,000 = $.05.

Now, for the press tour, let's assume that six of the placements that resulted from the press tour contained a key message and that the total circulation of the outlets in which those messages appeared was 1.5 million. Total opportunities to see a key message equals 6 x 1.5 million = 9 million. To get CPMC, divide 9 million into $50,000: $50,000 ÷ 9,000,000 = $.006.

Therefore, the press tour had a lower CPMC and was more efficient at communicating key messages.

the advertising CPMC are the same. However, experience has shown that only about 20 percent of PR placements actually contain a key message. That is, of all the articles that result from your press release and mention your company, only about one fifth of them will include one of your company's key messages.

In practice, the actual percent of articles that include key messages varies greatly from case to case. Therefore, you must examine your placements during the time period in question and determine which ones contain your key messages. Some may contain more than one key message. For each article, multiply the number of key messages by the circulation figure of the publication(s) in which the article appeared to get the number of opportunities to see your key messages for that article. Add up all the opportunities to see key messages for all the articles in the time period, and that figure is your total opportunities to see a key message:

total opportunities to see a key message =
(number of key messages in article #1) x (circulation of article #1)
+ (number of key messages in article #2) x (circulation of article #2)
+ (number of key messages in article #3) x (circulation of article #3)
+ ... and so on for all articles

Next, take your total PR costs for the time period and divide it by total opportunities to see a key message to get the cost per opportunity to see a key message, or cost per message communicated, CPMC:

total PR costs ÷ total opportunities to see a key message = CPMC

This is particularly effective when you are trying to compare the effectiveness of different communications tactics such as events, press conferences, press tours, and the like.

PRV: PR Value Ratio

If you would like to show the relative value of PR compared to advertising, look at how well both techniques promote the overall goals of your program. If your goal is to use earned media to promote the key messages or the agenda of the organization, then it makes sense to compare the reach and frequency of your message communication with that of advertising.

For example, if research reveals that your earned media has reached a million pairs of eyeballs with your messages, that would be a significant milestone. More importantly, if it reached those million eyeballs at a fraction of the cost of buying the same

---

A Note About Comparisons with Advertising

One might argue—and I frequently do—that ads contain certain things that most article placements don't. Specifically, they almost always include product photos or other images, brand benefits, and detailed descriptions of brand features. Thus an ad is generally highly favorable to a product and/or company, but an article is *not* always favorable.

So if your intent is to compare advertising with some other marketing vehicle, it makes sense to count only favorable articles when adding up the other marketing vehicle's results. Depending on your purpose and the data you have available, you may decide to only include in your analysis those articles that contain either a photo, a key message, a statement of brand benefits, or a description of brand features. Do not include negative or neutral articles, or those that don't contain key messages.

---

eyeballs with advertising, you would have proof that PR was contributing in a big way to the organization's bottom line.

So, for example, if the annual PR budget is $100,000 and the ad budget is $1 million, and both deliver the organization's key messages to 5 million eyeballs a year, PR delivers the same output for a tenth of the cost. The PR to advertising value ratio, or PRV, would be 10:1.

Cost per Minute Spent with Customer

Sometimes you have to be a bit more creative about what you benchmark against. Instead of making comparisons based on cost per impression, it can be useful to compare cost per minute spent with a customer. The pharmaceutical industry figures that it costs about $300 to get a sales representative in front of a doctor for five minutes. That's a cost per minute of $300 ÷ 5 = $60. Getting a minute of that same doctor's time at a trade show costs about $25. A black-and-white ad in the *Journal of the American Medical Association*, which appears only once and gets a doctor's attention

---

Calculating PR to Advertising Value Ratio, PRV

Consider a typical KDPaine & Partners client, which places or earns 1,000 articles a year. Of those articles, about 30 percent, or 300, contain the company's key messages. Of those 300, typically 80 percent, or 240, appear in publications that reach the target audience. For the sake of this example, let's assume that the audited circulation figures of the publications in which those 240 articles appeared add up to 5 million eyeballs that have seen the client's key messages.

Let's say the company's annual PR budget is $100,000; we divide that by 5 million and get a cost per key message communicated (CPMC) of $.02. To compare that with advertising, it has to be expressed in the way advertising typically does, as cost per thousand people reached. Multiply the CPMC of $.02 by 1,000 to get a CPM of $20.

Let's now assume that the advertising budget is $1 million a year and according to the media plan, the combined reach and frequency resulted in 5 million people seeing the organization's key messages via paid advertising. Assuming that every ad contains a key message, they've reached 5 million people with their key messages via advertising. That's a CPM of $200.

In this example, PR has delivered the same number of key messages to eyeballs for a tenth of the cost, or a PRV of 10:1.

---

for maybe 20 seconds, has a cost per minute price tag of about $66. But what if that pharmaceutical company was spending $200,000 a year on its website, and that doctor (one of say 50,000 who visited the website in a year) was enticed to spend five minutes on the site? Cost per minute spent with a doctor drops to $.80.

Comparing GRPs

Another frequently used measurement term in the television advertising world is GRP, or gross rating points. One rating point represents one percent of the population base you are trying to reach. So if the television show *Lost* has a GRP of 10, it is reaching 10 percent of the U.S. population, or roughly 100 million viewers.

Because GRP is such a frequently used advertising term, it is tempting to use it to compare results with media relations. This can work particularly well if you are in the consumer packaged-goods field. We made use of this technique when working for Procter & Gamble's hair care and cosmetics business unit. It wanted to be able to quickly determine if it was doing better or worse over time, so it asked my company to create a dashboard.

Procter & Gamble has done enough advertising and market research over the years to know how many eyeballs it needs to reach in order to sell a case of shampoo. It also knows that the most compelling components of an ad are a visual of the product, an endorsement, and a list of the benefits that the product offers. So if a story in the beauty care section of *Harpers Bazaar* mentions Max Factor lipstick, contains a photograph of the product or a model wearing the lipstick, mentions a brand benefit and encourages the reader to try it, Procter & Gamble assumes that a reader would be as compelled to try the product as she would be if she were reading an ad. It then looks at what other publications also ran stories that contained recommendations, brand benefits, and photographs. Then it uses audited circulation figures to calculate the total number of women who had the opportunity to see those articles in each of the publications during the month.

For example, let's assume there were 10 stories that contained those elements in publications with circulations that add up to 16 million. Instead of comparing PR to advertising by way of a print ad measure (like CPM), let's use the TV ad measure, GRP. Sixteen million represents 16 percent of the women in the U.S., or, say, the TV ratings equivalent of *Desperate Housewives*. So Procter & Gamble assumes it will sell as many tubes of lipstick as it would by advertising on *Desperate Housewives*. It can then compare the cost of producing and placing the ad with the cost of placing the articles to get an idea of which generates more sales per dollar invested (see PR Value Ratio, page 74).

Procter & Gamble knows that marketing doesn't happen in a vacuum, so it also compares its share of recommendations, photos, and brand benefit mentions to its main competitors.

In developing Procter & Gamble's dashboard, we knew from previous data that it was harder to earn recommendations from editors than it was to simply get brand benefits into a story. So we weighted the different elements according to the difficulty of generating each one and created a composite score that reflected the success achieved relative to the competition.

While this example might appear to be specific to a consumer packaged-goods company, there are elements that translate to any business. If you understand what drives customer behavior, and you understand how PR affects those drivers, then you can measure PR's impact on customer behavior. What you're doing is comparing marketing techniques through sales.

1. Start with the elements that drive the desired customer behavior. In cosmetics it was seeing brand benefits, brand photographs, and brand recommendations. In the different case of a major medical clinic, it knows that what motivates patients to come to the clinic is the recommendations of its doctors and their families, as well as the perception that the clinic's physicians are experts and that the clinic is the *only* place they can get that level of care. So it measures its media success by its share of stories that contain doctor's quotes and/or position the clinic as the best place a patient can get a specific procedure or specific types of surgery.

2. Measure success against the competition so you aren't measuring in a vacuum. You need to know how well you are doing relative to the competition, not just yourself.

3. Don't look at clip counts, but look instead at the percentage of the total target audience you have reached.

4. Factor the desired customer behavior into your measures of success.

Chapter 6

Measuring Trust and Mistrust

It is error only, and not truth, that shrinks from inquiry.
—Thomas Paine

Trust, or lack thereof, has a measurable effect on the financial health of an organization. The accounting firm Arthur Anderson was destroyed after the Enron scandal because its clients lost their trust in its results. Whenever news of tainted beef hits the airwaves consumers lose trust in the safety of their favorite burger and fast food sales take a dive. Conversely, a key to FedEx's success is that customers trust the company's pledge to deliver "When it absolutely, positively has to be there" overnight.

When trust helps an organization build relationships with key constituencies, it saves that organization money by reducing the costs of litigation, regulation, legislation, pressure campaigns, boycotts, or lost revenue that result from bad relationships. A high level of trust helps cultivate relationships with donors, consumers, investors, and legislators who are needed to support organizational goals. When employees trust their employer they are more likely to support the mission of the organization and be satisfied with their jobs. Lower employee turnover has a direct impact on the bottom line. Trust from the financial community is critical to an organization's access to capital and therefore its ability to grow. Good relationships with the media can often avert a crisis.

Typical Outputs, Outtakes, and Outcomes for Measuring Trust

Outputs: Number of times your brand is mentioned as trustworthy by the media

Outtakes: Change in perception of your organization as a trustworthy organization

Outcomes: Percent change in number of people that reinvest in your company and/or become repeat purchasers

---

Even though examples such as these make it clear that trust is important, few companies actually measure the trust that their constituencies have in them. This chapter provides guidelines, generated with the help of the Institute for Public Relations, for helping organizations measure the degree to which their customers or constituencies trust them. See Appendix 2 for more references on trust measurement.

What Is Trust?

Trust has been a widely studied concept both by itself and, most importantly, as a component of the quality of relationships. Research by Jim Grunig and Linda Hon (see Appendix 1) has shown that trust is one of six independently measurable components of relationships. Two of the other components are *exchange* and *communal*, each with its own relationship to trust:

- *Exchange relationship*: In an exchange relationship, one party gives benefits to the other only because the other has provided benefits in the past or is expected to do so in the future. Exchange is the essence of marketing relationships between organizations and customers and is the central concept of marketing theory. Many relationships begin as exchange relationships and then develop into communal relationships as they mature. Often, mutually beneficial exchanges can begin to build trust, but exchange relationships never develop the same levels of trust that accompanies communal relationships.

- *Communal relationship*: All parties in a communal relationship provide benefits to each other because they are concerned for the welfare of the other, even when they get nothing in return. Communal relationships are essential to developing and enhancing trust in an organization. Communal relationships are important if organizations are to be socially responsible and add value to society as well as to client organizations. They also greatly reduce the likelihood of negative behaviors from stakeholders.

The Grunig Trust Dimensions

Research on trust has shown that it is a multi-dimensional concept. Jim Grunig has identified three dimensions of trust that are measurable by the Grunig Relationship Survey (see Appendix 1):

- *Competence*: The belief that an organization has the ability to do what it says it will do, including the extent to which an organization is seen as being effective, and that it can compete and survive in the marketplace;

- *Integrity*: The belief that an organization is fair and just;

- *Dependability/reliability*: The belief that an organization will do what it says it will do, that it acts consistently and dependably.

Other Components of Trust

Although the experts are not in complete agreement, trust between an organization and its publics is generally described as having the following independently quantifiable characteristics:

- *Multilevel*: Trust results from interactions that span coworker, team, organizational, and interorganizational alliances, which is why you need to cast a wide net when you survey your publics on trust.

- *Culturally-rooted*: Trust is closely tied to the norms, values, and beliefs of the organizational culture. Therefore it is critical to understand the self-image and self-definitions of your publics if you are going to accurately measure trust.

- *Communication-based*: Trust is the outcome of communications behaviors, such as providing accurate information, giving explanations for decisions, and demonstrating sincere and appropriate openness, which is why communications metrics are critical in trust measurement.

- *Dynamic*: Trust is constantly changing as it cycles through phases of building, destabilization, and dissolving, so it is important to measure trust on a continuum over time.

- *Multidimensional*: Trust consists of multiple factors at the cognitive, emotional, and behavioral levels, all of which affect an individual's perceptions of trust.

Tucker's Three Varieties of Trust

Just to add another wrinkle to this discussion, Andrew Tucker, in a paper delivered at the 2006 International Public Relations Research Conference (IPRRC), postulated three measurable varieties of trust:

- *Short term trust*, which is based on financial performance and product quality metrics like *Fortune*'s Most Admired list;

- *Medium term trust* (which he calls "reflexive mistrust"), which translates roughly to, "I can't totally trust you

because I don't know you, but I need to trust you somewhat to do my job or fill my need";

- *Long-term trust*, which is based on customer loyalty.

Reflexive Trust

I believe that there's another variety of trust, something I call
"reflexive trust." That's the situation in which a source loses its
trustworthiness because of frequent obfuscation or spin, and as
a result an opposing or contradictory source takes on greater
trustworthiness. As an example, while listening to an interview
on the BBC last night with representatives from Hamas, I realized
that my usual skeptical response was flipped around, and I actually had more faith in what the Hamas representative had to say
than what the representative of the U.S. government was saying.
That was because, to my mind at least, the U.S. government had
been lying so consistently about events in the Middle East that
in addition to losing its own credibility, it had provided a sort of
reverse recommendation to any opposing view. There's a lesson
in this for many organizations: If you consistently obfuscate, lie,
and spin, at some point your very statements begin to enhance
your competitor's—or enemy's—credibility.

Trust, Bullshit, and the Truth

That's exactly what Brad Rawlins and Kevin Stoker were talking about in their 2006 IPRRC paper on BS in PR. Their point
was that bullshit is more damaging than lies. Liars, they argue,
have a fundamental respect for—or at least knowledge of—the
truth, and they choose not to use it. Bullshitters (and, I argue,
those who spin PR), on the other hand, use language to blur the
truth, and are intentionally careless and vague about the truth.
He cites the book *On Bullshit*, by Henry G. Frankfurt (Princeton
University Press, 2005). Frankfurt's point is that bullshit isn't
false, it's fake. Its intent is not to mislead about facts but about

impressions and to create favorable impressions despite unfavorable facts.

Rawlins and Stoker argue that bullshit is insidious not because the person speaking the bullshit believes it, but because he or she is trying to manipulate people with it. They claim we need to change this environment and inject more honesty, loyalty, and moral values into what we say and write as part of our profession. In this new era of transparency, your target audience is putting greater emphasis on character value. To increase your trust and credibility, make sure that the things you do and the things you espouse and believe in are the same. Rawlins argues that this is good strategy–not just a virtuous model–and that organizations need to take responsibility for their actions.

Even more important, he argues that a PR professional can't blame bullshit on the organization, and that it comes down to personal integrity. The bottom line is, according to Rawlins: hold on to the virtue. Abandon the vices. Get rid of the disconnects between what you believe and what you do. Work for organizations that have character in the way they operate, in their visions and values. If the organization doesn't have character, and hasn't changed its character to correct a crisis, then you are communicating bullshit. "You have to be willing to say the things that no one wants to hear," said Rawlins. His final point—which returns to my point about reflexive trust—is that if everything we say is tainted by bullshit, no one will believe anything we try to communicate.

Trust Measurement

Trust measurement and evaluation involves assessing the success or failure of an organization's effort to improve and enhance its relationships with key constituents. More specifically, trust measurement is a way of giving a result a precise specification, generally by comparison to some standard or baseline, and usually is done in a quantifiable or numerical manner. It seeks to answer questions such as:

- Have the behaviors, programs, and activities we implemented changed what people know, think, and feel about the organization, and how they actually act (as exhibited by protests, votes, and purchases)?

- Have the actions or behaviors of our organization had an effect on the trust that our constituencies feel toward our organization?

- Have the public relations and communications efforts that were initiated to build trust had an effect? If so, how can we support and document that with research?

As with any measurement program, trust measurement involves the steps described in Chapter 1, although somewhat altered for this application.

Step 1: Define Your Publics

Identify those groups or individuals with whom your organization has or needs relationships. Once these publics have been identified, you can begin to create a system to measure the degree to which each trusts your organization.

Step 2: Set Specific, Measurable Goals and Objectives

No one can really measure the effectiveness of anything without first figuring out exactly what it is they are measuring. The communications practitioner, counselor, and/or research supplier ought to ask: What are or were the goals or objectives of the organization? What exactly did the program or the activities hope to accomplish? The more specific the answers, the more meaningful the research will be. For example: Trust will be increased by 10 percent in 2010."

Step 3: Select a Measurement Tool

There is no one, simple, all-encompassing research tool, technique or methodology you can rely on to measure and evaluate trust. You will usually need to devise a combination of different measurement techniques appropriate for your company or client. Some of the tools and techniques to measure trust include:

- Surveys
- Focus groups
- Before-and-after polls
- Ethnographic studies
- Experimental and quasi-experimental designs
- Multivariate analysis projects
- Model building

To measure the perceptions of an organization's relationships with key constituencies, focusing on the elements of trust as defined above, we suggest administering a questionnaire that includes a series of agree/disagree statements pertaining to the relationship, such as those of the Grunig Relationship Survey (see Appendix 1). Respondents are asked to use a 1-to-7 scale to indicate the extent to which they agree or disagree that each item listed describes their relationship with that particular organization.

Over the long term, the value of increasing the level of trust in your organization can be measured in money saved from lower costs of expansion, lower litigation fees, lower costs of recruitment and, ultimately, lower cost of operations.

Step 4: Analyze Results

First identify any opposition to management goals and decisions before it results in a crisis or develops into an issue with your constituencies. Second, use your data to help management understand that certain decisions might have adverse consequences on the public's trust. Recent research by Brad Rawlins implies that greater organizational transparency tends to build trust, while less transparency tends to diminish it. With data in hand, management might make different decisions and behave differently than otherwise.

There are many times when improved trust or relationships do not lead to immediate changes in behavior, so it is important to set realistic expectations. Trust and good relationships keep publics from engaging in negative behaviors such as litigation, strikes, protests, or negative publicity. It is very difficult to measure a behavior that did not occur because of a good relationship. If a controversy never hits the media as a result of relationship building efforts, and if you are only measuring media relations, there will be no statistical evidence that your relationship building efforts worked.

One way around this is to interview members of the community to test their perceptions. Another way to approach it is to look at your organization's share of negatives as compared to that of peer companies or competitors. If your share of negatives is declining while the others' are holding steady or going up, you know your strategy is working.

At other times, there may be a long lead time between the development of a good relationship and a behavior. For example, if you make a habit of inviting members of a community to social events and other relationship-building occasions, they may see you as friendlier or nicer or easier to deal with. As a result, you are more likely to find that differences or misunderstandings between that audience and your organization can be resolved by conversations rather than litigation. However, it may take months or, more likely, years before your social efforts have a measurable effect on legal fees.

Chapter 7

Measuring the Impact of Events and Sponsorships on Your Public Relationships

One of the great mistakes is to judge policies and programs by their intentions rather than their results.

—Milton Friedman

In the future, most purchasing will be neatly divided into two categories: online and experiential. Decisions will be based on familiarity with the brand and ease of ordering, relatively new concepts to most traditional retailers. Nike gets it, as does Victoria's Secret and Borders Books. Now, I'm an avid Amazon fan, but I still go into Borders' brick-and-mortar stores and end up buying something. Why? Because I get to touch, feel, browse, and listen to products in those rare hours when I have nothing else to do. If I *need* something in a hurry, I go online. If I want "retail therapy," I go to Borders, Anthropologie, or my local antique store.

How Are People Involved with Your Brand?

Which brings us back to the importance of knowing something more than just how many eyeballs saw your brand, or how many people walked by your booth or display. A far more valuable measure is how many people are somehow engaged with your brand or your organization: What is the nature and strength of that relationship?

**Typical Outputs, Outtakes, and Outcomes
for Measuring Events and Sponsorships**

Outputs: Number of times your brand is mentioned in conjunction with an event or sponsorship

Outtakes: Percent of attendees who remember your brand or your sponsorship

Outcomes: Percent of attendees who visit a dealership, showroom, store and/or website

In his seminal book *Lovemarks*, Kevin Roberts, CEO of Saatchi and Saatchi, describes how we develop relationships with the brands we love. Roberts argues that if a brand offers mystery, sensuality, and intimacy, it has the makings of a Lovemark. I would argue that Lovemarks are all about building and nurturing relationships around a brand.

In fact, a 2006 study by Jack Morton Worldwide found that live event marketing—experiences where consumers interact with products, brands, or "brand ambassadors" face-to-face—are among the most effective ways to influence coveted consumer audiences. The study, an online survey of 2,574 consumers between the ages of 13 and 65 in the top 25 U.S. markets, confirmed that this increasingly important marketing medium resonates strongly across all demographic and product categories.

So sponsorships, events, and other word-of-mouth programs have taken on a far more critical role than ever before. But it is no longer enough to simply measure the number of eyeballs reached by a bunch of banners or t-shirts. Today's savvy marketers are demanding much more than CPM numbers (as useful as they may be in comparing cost efficiencies across different media and tactics, see Chapter 5). They are looking to measure the relationships they are developing, both in terms of attitude change and also in terms of buying and behaviors.

This chapter is not about evaluating customer satisfaction or customer loyalty. There are lots of companies out there that can do that for you. Although you can certainly use customer satisfaction scores as a measure of success—and part of the standard relationship survey questionnaire does include a measure of satisfaction—product performance, price, and service have far more influence over customer satisfaction than does communications. Satisfaction is best measured by repeat purchases and the actual transactions that satisfied customers are making, not their response to a specific event.

As for most other audiences, measurement programs for sponsorships and events follow the basic steps described in Chapter 1.

Steps 1 and 2: Understand the Audience and Objectives

As with any effort, you can't start to measure success until you know what success means for you. To help people clarify their objectives, we surveyed corporate communications professionals to see what they thought was the number-one objective for their PR programs. Eighty-five percent cited product or corporate awareness as the number-one objective. Other typical objectives included the following:

- Increase exposure for the company name or product
- Increase dissemination of company or product messages
- Educate certain publics
- Generate leads
- Move prospects along the purchase cycle
- Sell product

Each objective, of course, requires a different type of measurement. Some types isolate the effect of PR from other communications efforts better than others. And the best objectives are specific and measurable. For any given event, specific goals might be:

- Increase in awareness
- Increase in preference
- Increase in purchase intent
- Increase in customer loyalty
- Percent improvement in customer experience

Step 3: Determine Measurable Criteria of Success

Once you've agreed upon your objectives, establish the specific criteria of success that you will measure. If your objective is awareness, the criterion might be the percentage increase of unaided awareness of brand or product. If your objective is to sell product, your criterion might be the incremental sales or traffic to local dealers after a particular PR or promotional program took place.

Consider those numbers that best reflect the health of your business, or that best represent customer characteristics that most affect your business:

- Percent of attendees more likely to purchase
- Percent of attendees remembering the brand
- Number of qualified sales leads generated
- Conversion rate of attendees
- Total potential sales (number of attendees x conversion rate x average sale)
- For press events: number of key editors and analysts attending
- Percent of attendees writing on or quoted on the issue
- Total exposure of key messages in resulting press

To a certain extent, your choice of criteria is dependent on the type of event you are evaluating. If the customer experience you are measuring takes place at a trade show or exhibit booth, you might choose as key criteria the percentage of new visitors or the cost per minute spent with a client in the booth. If the experience takes place at an event such as a concert, you need to count how many people were exposed to your brand or the brand experience you were offering. Don't trust the promoter's numbers, do your own counting. I often follow up with a survey to see if the brand was remembered.

The Case of the Unfocused Auto Manufacturer

I met with a major auto manufacturer who wanted to measure the effectiveness of different sponsorships. It was spending many millions sponsoring car races, golf tournaments, antique car auctions, and a variety of other events. I asked the assembled executives what they were trying to achieve by these efforts. The first response was essentially: "We are a major sponsor of these types of events." Finally, after about two hours of discussion, we agreed that the business objective was to drive potential customers into dealer showrooms.

We began a series of surveys at each event to determine first if the attendees remembered the sponsors and second if they were more or less likely to test drive and/or buy the auto manufacturer's car. We collected names at the event itself and called attendees two weeks after the event. Our results showed that, on average, 50 percent of all attendees were more likely to test drive one of the sponsor's vehicles after attending the event. After we had measured several events, we were able to compare and contrast the cost effectiveness (dollars per person reached) of different events. See Figure 9, page 95.

These results led the auto manufacturer to alter its sponsorship strategies dramatically and focus more on golf and antique car events, rather than traditional car races. It also enabled the sponsor to better understand the ROI from each event. By looking at the percentage of people more likely to go to a dealership, it

---

Country Music Television Tunes in to Their Viewers

Country Music Television (CMT) had a program of Wal-Mart parking lot music events, which would move from location to location in tractor trailers. Prior to contacting us it had measured results by asking the truck drivers how many people showed up. Realizing that this might not be the most accurate methodology, it contracted with my company to design measurement for these events.

CMT's stated purpose was to convince attendees to call their local cable company and request CMT, or to take some other action on behalf of CMT. We agreed with CMT that the common criterion against which we should measure all events was an *adhoc* measure we called "level of engagement." This was defined as the average response of attendees, on a scale of 1 to 5, when asked how much the parking lot event affected their relationship with CMT. We further defined success as an increase in the percentage of people willing to take action on behalf of CMT. A sweatshirt giveaway was included at the events to collect names and addresses of attendees, and we surveyed a sample of these people by phone two weeks after the event.

Our surveys showed that 93 percent of attendees were willing to take some action and 89 percent were willing to make a phone call to their local cable company. We then compared results between different events in different cities so CMT could determine where to expand the program the following year.

---

could determine the number of potential buyers. By subtracting the cost of the sponsorship from the profit and the projected number of car sales, it determined a projected ROI from the event. See Figure 10, page 96.

But it's important to look beyond simple quantitative data, especially if your objective is exposure, to assess the *quality* of your communications. Do they remember being in your booth? Did they even know you were a sponsor? Did they remember your brand, and the brand benefits or brand positioning you were trying to convey? Did they leave more likely to purchase or to recommend?

When companies clearly define their objectives it becomes a relatively simple matter to define a set of criteria against which we can measure the company's relationships with its constitu-

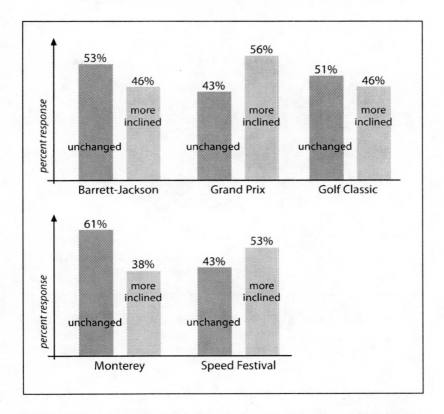

Figure 9. Percent attendee response to: "After the event, did you feel more or less likely to visit the showroom of the sponsor?"

encies in different events. Then it is possible to compare and contrast results consistently across a number of different events to ensure that the company has the most effective sponsorship program possible.

Step 4: Decide Upon a Benchmark

The key point to remember about any evaluation program is that measurement is a comparative tool: you need to compare one set

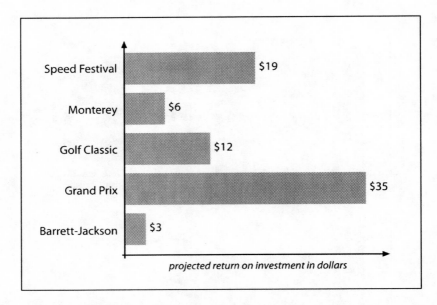

Figure 10. Comparing events with projected ROI. Event results varied greatly.

of results to something else. The most meaningful comparisons are between different events, or between you and competing sponsors at one event.

Step 5: Select a Measurement Tool

In our opinion, the most reliable way to measure relationships with your customers is to conduct an in-depth phone survey using the Grunig Relationship Survey (see Appendix 1). This instrument has been thoroughly tested and shown to be an extremely effective measure of how customers perceive their relationships with an organization. The Grunig survey instrument includes a number of statements to which respondents are asked if they agree or disagree. Some example statements are:

- This organization treats people like me fairly and justly.

- This organization can be relied on to keep its promises.

- I believe that this organization takes the opinions of people like me into account when making decisions.

- I feel very confident about this organization's skills.

If your organization has neither the means nor the resources to conduct an in-depth relationship study by phone, there are several alternatives. Online surveys are most organizations' first choice these days. While they do suffer from self-selecting samples, the advantages of low cost and quick turnaround are hard to beat. They are particularly effective in measuring relationships with members of an organization that are all on a listserve of some sort (see Chapter 13, "Measuring Relationships with Members of Your Organization"). If you are evaluating an event, the first option that most people consider is an on-site in-person survey, which is not recommended unless you are only interested in people's immediate reactions. Of far more value is an understanding of their takeaways—their longer-term perceptions and memories, which are much more effectively gathered after the event via a phone or email survey.

Our own research bears this out. We have conducted numerous trade show surveys both on-site and after events, with our samples always comprised of people who actually visit a booth. Typically, about 20 percent of people surveyed after the show (and, remember, these are people who had to be in the booth for us to get their names) do not recall visiting the booth at all. We find that whatever people *do* remember after the show is of greater value than their on-site responses, when they are often most concerned about their sore feet.

For example, data from post-show surveys is far more revealing and reliable about purchase intent. If you ask an event attendee at a show if he or she is likely to purchase a product, chances are they'll say yes just to make the interviewer happy. But if you call after the fact and ask if they have purchased or intend to purchase, the response is far more likely to reflect reality. Remember, however, that in event measurement time is of the essence. You need the data in time to make decisions—and typically those decisions are made fairly quickly after an event is concluded.

Another alternative to the on-site or post-show survey is to closely track website traffic before, during, and after an event, to determine if there are any significant changes as a result of the event. If you are a consumer packaged-goods company, you can use scanning data to track sales impact. Colgate Palmolive sponsored the Starlight Starbright Children's Foundation and promoted it in point of sale communications for several specific brands. It then tracked the sell-through of those brands after the sponsorship was launched. As it turns out, the sponsorship was very cost effective for some of its brands, but had little impact on others.

The final steps for sponsorship and event measurement follow steps six and seven as outlined in Chapter 1.

Chapter 8

Measuring Relationships with Your Local Community

All business in a democratic society begins with public permission and exists by public approval.

—Arthur W. Page

Too often, organizations think of their publics as only their customers and the thought leaders of the industry. Not until there is picketing at the gates do they wake up and realize that there are other publics they need to get permission and approval from. So they designate someone to "do community relations"—a few speeches at the Rotary Club, some United Way activities, and a flurry of self-congratulatory press releases—and then they assume that their relationships with the neighbors are just fine, thank you. It's not until a permit is denied, a key vote is lost, or the protesters are back at the gates that someone wonders whether all that time and money spent on the community relations department was worth anything.

Who Are Your Neighbors and Why Are They Important?

Like measuring any other public relationship, gauging the strength or weakness of your reputation among your neighbors must start with a list of all the publics you are trying to influence. "Community" is way too general a term for our purpose here; the community is often made up of very disparate elements. For instance, I live in the little town of Durham, New Hampshire,

---

**Typical Outputs, Outtakes, and Outcomes
for Measuring Community Relationships**

Outputs: Share of coverage in local papers: number of articles, tone of articles (positive, negative, neutral), key messages

Outtakes: The percentage of the community that sees you as trustworthy, credible, reliable, and/or committed to the community

Outcomes: Changes in legal and recruitment costs, changes in number or severity of labor disputes

---

home to some 7,500 other souls. Durham is also the home of the University of New Hampshire, and many of my fellow community members attend the university. Although technically I am a part of the Durham community, there are a great many other members of the community with whom I have very little in common—the ones that drink excessive quantities of beer, burn their mattresses in the street, and then pass out on fraternity lawns, for example. Just because they are students doesn't mean that their votes or their opinions are any less worthy of attention, they just need a slightly different type of attention.

Step 1: Your Audience Is Your Neighbors

Start by making a detailed list of all the segments of the community; include elected and appointed officials, heads of local special interest groups, and anyone else who might influence public perceptions of your organization. These key stakeholders are your audience.

Step 2: How Do Good or Bad Relationships Influence Your Organization?

If they're on your list of key stakeholders, they can either help or hurt your cause. Itemize exactly how a good relationship helps

Influencer	Impact or Benefit
Elected officials	Can withhold or grant permission to expand/build
Official wannabes and candidates	Can make a campaign issue out of your plans
Customers	Contribute to revenue
Noncustomers	Potential customers, potential employees
NGOs	Influence elected officials, have the ear of the local media
Town staff	Can create or reduce paper work, grant approvals
Local radio and TV reporters	Primary source of news for local community
Local print reporters	Read by influentials, source of opinion
Senior citizens	Votes, volunteers
Students	Votes, volunteers, future employees, future customers
Academics	Opinion leaders, source of interns, research supplier
Merchants	Potential customers
Opinion leaders	Source of opinion, votes
Other influentials	Recommenders
Bloggers	Read by the media and influentials, source of opinion

Table 7. Community influencers, and how a good or bad relationship with each group impacts your organization.

and a bad relationship threatens your reputation. See Table 7 on page 101.

Step 3: Who and What Is Most Important to Measure?

Assume you will be able, at least at first, to measure at most three to five of these groups, and that the audiences that are the most important will get surveyed first. For each audience, determine at least one measure of a successful relationship. It could be out-puts (for example, the number of your stories that show up in the local paper), outtakes (for example, the percent of students that perceive you to be the employer of choice in the area) or outcomes (such as percent increase in qualified applicants for jobs or volunteer positions).

Step 4: Who or What Are Your Benchmarks?

Since measurement is a comparison tool, you will need to compare the strength of your community relations to something or someone else. It could be to other communities (such as other towns where you may have a plant or office) or, better yet, to peer companies within the same community. So you select one or two peer organizations, of similar size and reputation. For example, when we studied the reputation in the local community of a major corporation in Minneapolis, we chose to compare against a department store and a food producer, both of which were comparably charitable and comparably visible in the community. In another example, when an international airline wanted to gauge its relationship with the local media, we compared local media coverage to coverage of the same airline in other cities around the country.

One of the problems in finding another organization with which to compare your results is that so many organizations are the only game in town. Ordinarily, you'd like to be able to benchmark against your direct competition, but the chances of having a competing company or organization in the same neighborhood are pretty slim. In my town of Durham, for example, the University of New Hampshire is by far the dominant institution. In these cases, to find an appropriate benchmark you may need to go outside your local community and team up with your peers at comparable organizations in comparable communities elsewhere. Nonprofits and education institutions frequently take this approach, and it has the added benefit of helping to reduce your research costs. Remember, however, to do your best to compare apples to apples; for the University of New Hampshire another state school in a small town would probably be an appropriate benchmark, but a private school in a large urban center would not.

Step 5: What Are the Most Appropriate Measurement Tools?

Once you've decided what other organizations or communities you are benchmarking against, you select your measurement tools. In general, if your key source of influence are the local media, you will want to monitor it with media content analysis. This involves collecting articles and mentions from all the local news outlets: TV, radio, online, weekly papers, dailies, and if possible, any listserves, community email newsletters, or blogs. (For a more detailed discussion of media content analysis, see Chapter 2.) Make sure you are a subscriber to every source of news in the area, or, if you've hired a clipping agency, make sure it is tracking them all for you.

The importance of local email lists and online publications cannot be overemphasized. The ease with which they pass along articles and opinions can be a key factor in rallying supporters and protestors. Here in Durham what started out as a small meeting of friends became a 2,000-person politics-oriented mailing list that has elected conservation-oriented candidates, stopped the construction of a major sports complex (see the example in the Preface), blocked a number of housing developments, and become one of the biggest local sources of influential opinion.

If your objective is to improve relationships with members of the local community, analyzing the media is just the first step in the process. While it is important to understand what people are reading and seeing about you in the news, it is far more important to gauge the strength (or weakness) of your relationship with them. See Appendix 1 on using the Grunig Relationship Survey and Chapter 6 on how to measure trust.

Step 6: Analyze the Data

The next step is to analyze the media content to determine whether or not your community messages are being communicated. Find residents of the local community to read and code the articles, because only they will respond to them as your target audience(s) would.

Remember, you should *not* be reading and analyzing the content yourself. First of all, most PR people can spot a key message a mile away, and secondly, we are generally news junkies and do not read articles like normal human beings. We spot nuances, recognize bylines, and generally read articles far more thoroughly than your average local resident does. And of course, chances are good that you are *not* a local resident, and cannot possibly understand what will or will not resonate with local residents.

Each article should be analyzed to determine to what extent the coverage is accurate, balanced, and fair. Are you getting more than your fair share of bad news? (That's why you want a peer organization to compare results with.) Track the source of each article: Was it generated by your department, or by someone else in the local community? Who was quoted in the article, and did that quote reflect your desired positioning or messages? How visible are you? Unlike in product PR, visibility at a local level is not necessarily desirable. It can make you a bigger target for protestors and for charitable organizations looking for corporate sponsors. I also recommend that you ask your readers to note how your organization is positioned in each article. Are you portrayed as an employer of choice or neighbor of choice? Are you described as concerned about the environment or the community?

Special Considerations for Measuring Local Relationships

When It Comes Up for a Vote, It's Too Late to Change Anything

If your objective is to create an environment in which expansion of your facility is welcome, the outcome of a critical vote is *not* a good measurement tool. Yes, a vote is an outcome, but once a motion comes before the town council or a local board, it is way too late to change anything. It can take 18 months to change people's minds on an issue, so don't wait until the month before a vote to launch the PR effort. Months before the vote is taken, you need to understand how officials and townspeople perceive your organization, how they feel about the issues, and where they stand. If possible, poll them regularly, once a month or once a quarter, to see how opinions fluctuate.

Fishing in the Talent Pool?

If your objective is to be the employer of choice within the commutable area (to ensure a readily available talent pool), keep tabs on requests for applications and responses to local ads. But just counting applications may not be enough. At least once a year you should survey the local community to find out how your organization is perceived as an employer. Again, use the Grunig instrument as discussed in Appendix 1.

Nonprofit Measures

If you are a nonprofit organization, amount of donations and numbers of volunteers are clearly logical measures of success. Measure these outcomes on a regular basis, because they are such important indicators that if they begin to decline you need to know immediately and determine why. When revenues fall, organizations too frequently blame "the economy" or some outside force without any facts to back up the assertion. Regular relationship surveys of your community can provide the information you need to determine not just why revenues are down, but how you can improve them.

Government Can Plan—and Poll—Ahead

If you are a government institution, bottom-line measures like revenues, donations, or applications may not apply. What most government institutions want from their local communities are cooperation, trust, and support at the polls. Again, if you wait until election day to measure results, it will be too late to change or influence the outcomes. Polling the community on a regular basis will help you gauge sentiment and influence it in time to make a difference.

Campus Opportunities

If you have a college or university in your community, you may find some assistance with your research. Academic institutions have an advantage that many other organization don't have—a genetic willingness to share information. Plus, they provide a built-in cadre of surveyors, researchers, and interns. If you are studying the local reputation of a college or university, chances are you can collaborate with other institutions to share costs.

Plan Ahead for a Crisis

It takes months to build up a reputation, and only a minute to destroy it in a crisis. It is critical is to understand the nature of your relationships *before* a crisis breaks. Then you can make necessary repairs well in advance, rather than operating in the dark in emergency conditions. Remember that you can manage relationships, but you can't manage reputation. You can't tell someone what to think and have them think that way, you can only manage the relationship in a way that enhances reputation.

Chapter 9

Measuring Internal Communications

We know that communication is a problem, but the company is not going to discuss it with the employees.
—Switching supervisor, AT&T Long Lines Division

Way back when nets were something our grandmothers wore to control their hair, and webs were where spiders hung out, companies had the mistaken notion that employees lived in glass bubbles. These employees obviously spoke a different language from anyone else on the planet; employee newsletters, videos, and internal communications departments all proved that. Somehow these workers were magically isolated from all other news sources and therefore could be spoon-fed only the news chosen by their employers.

In fact, many companies thought that *all* their audiences lived in bubbles: investors, the media, overseas markets, distributors, and sales people. Because of this, each individual department tried to communicate with these separate audiences by using different tools and different messages.

The Internet and other communications tools of the 21st century have changed all that. Today, employees are likely to get information about developments in your company from blogs, text messaging, wikis, and email. Media and information saturate our lives; with a few key strokes, everyone has access to exactly the same information. So companies are responding and restructuring. The typical PR or

Typical Outputs, Outtakes, and Outcomes for Measuring Internal Communications

Outputs: Number of targeted messages reaching employees each month or quarter

Outtakes: Percent of employees that believe in the mission and/or agree with management's messages

Outcomes: Change in turnover; change in cost of recruitment; change in percent of promotable employees

corporate communications manager I worked with 10 years ago now has responsibility for internal communications, investor relations, the company website, and international communications—in short, all of a company's possible constituencies.

Increasingly, the "employee communications" function is moving out of the human resources department and into communications. If the responsibility stays in HR, a professional communicator from corporate communications staffs it. Such staffing makes perfect sense because top management understands the value of corporate communication to the bottom line.

Here's the reason: top management recognizes more than the obvious benefits of HR communications. These communications include information about benefits, job openings, promotions, performance, productivity updates, company events, and so forth—all of which are of significant help to the functioning of the organization. However, top management also recognizes that a more strategically-focused dialogue with employees, one centered on meeting company objectives, can affect the bottom line more directly and importantly. For this reason companies need a skilled communicator with a full understanding of company direction, policy and procedure, structure, and goals.

It's not easy communicating to employees because they are already inundated with messages. Picture a typical employee who wakes up in the morning to NPR or talk radio, reads the local paper, talks to friends in a car pool, talks to coworkers around the water cooler, and reads a number of magazines and blogs relative to the job. On her way home, she sees ads at the grocery store and on the bus, talks to other parents at the children's football game, watches the evening news, helps her child play games on the Internet, checks out some of her favorite sites, reads a mommy blog or two, and then, having been bombarded with some 3,000 advertising messages along with countless other bits and bytes of information, sinks into a well-deserved slumber.

Somehow, amidst all that clutter, the boss is trying to communicate some gobbledygook about mission vision or values, or yet another option in a benefit plan. The chances of the message getting through to the employee are only slightly better than the chances of getting hit by a meteor.

Seven Steps to Measuring Internal Communication

So when did the last meteor hit? Forget whether employees like the internal newsletter. What you need to find out first is what messages even get through at all, how they're coming across, and through what media. A simple measurement program will provide this information, but it takes a corporate-wide commitment to implement. Internal measurement projects sometimes don't happen—or have their results ignored—because they get caught up in internal politics, maybe as a perceived threat to a fiefdom or as a casualty of an internal war between department heads. To successfully measure your company's relationship with its employees you must take these corporate politics into account and design your program to avoid pitfalls. So here are the seven steps necessary to get an internal communications measurement program in place.

Step 1: Understand the Environment and the Employees

A thorough, honest evaluation of existing communications—both official and unofficial sources of news and information—begins the process. Conduct a benchmark study using the appropriate tools from the section below, or with data that is already available somewhere in the organization. This initial benchmark study may be more or less involved depending on the size and complexity of the organization, on what measurement tools are already being used, and on what data is already available.

Collect and analyze all the various news bites, rumors, and pieces of electronic as well as nonelectronic documentation that regularly bombard your employees. You're looking for:

- What messages are getting through to employees?
- How are the messages getting across?
- What media are employees using to get the information?

Segment the Audience

Look around any company Christmas party and you'll quickly realize that employees are hardly a single audience. You'll see long-time employees and newbies, men and women, geeks and marketers, telecommuters and cubicle dwellers, branch office and main office. So don't measure them as if they're one group. Make sure you segment the audience as precisely as you can.

Determine What's Important to Them

Some 40 years ago, in a keynote address to the Advertising Club of St. Louis, Ralph Delahaye Paine, the editor of *Fortune,* mused, "If we can put a man in orbit, why can't we determine the effectiveness of our communications? The reason is simple and perhaps, therefore, a little old-fashioned: people, human beings with a wide range of choice. Unpredictable, cantankerous, capricious, motivated by innumerable conflicting interests, and conflicting desires."

In the ensuing years, we have developed increasingly effective methods to measure people's capriciousness, but the reality remains that humans still hear what they want to hear. How they determine what they want to hear is based upon what's important to them, perhaps what constitutes their most pressing and unfulfilled desires. If I need a new refrigerator because my old one broke down, I will be particularly receptive to news about and ads for appliances. The same goes for your employees. If their biggest concerns revolve around the health of the company and job security, then your messages about vision, values, and health care benefits will hardly register on them. If a number of pregnancies exist in a particular department, then those benefit messages will be picked up on first—you can bet on it.

Understand Where They Really Get Information

Of course we'd like employees to learn everything from "official" sources, but that just isn't going to happen. So where do they really get information and what formats are effective? Use your research to find out the influence of individual sources of information. Chat around the watercooler or coffeepot is probably a valuable source for some news; the company newsletter and company email is important for other types of information.

Child development researchers have discovered that different children learn in different ways. Some respond more readily to shapes and colors, others learn verbally from words and pictures, while still others learn aurally. To get all the children in a classroom to learn the same thing at the same time requires a cornucopia of teaching tools.

Caterpillar, Inc., the tractor company, learned this lesson with regard to its internal communications program. The company was accustomed to communicating internally in half a dozen different ways, but found that it could never quite reach everyone all the time; some group of employees always remained uninformed. Consequently, Caterpillar decided to put out the same news in every format, and has found dramatic increases in employee knowledge of corporate messages. Different employees prefer different media for different types of news.

Get Them to Tell You What They Think

Existing perceptions play an enormous role in whether or not employees will receive whatever messages you're trying to communicate. If you don't know the health and strength of your relationship, you have no idea whether they're likely to listen to what you have to say. And then, given the nature of the relationship, you still need to get them to tell you if they understand the vision and values: Do they have an understanding of what the company is trying to do?

In some companies we find that the space between line workers and management opens to such an extent that internal communicators need to start by educating employees about what business the company is in. Other companies are at the opposite end of the scale, using open-book management to keep every employee informed of not just the company business, but the actual financial details of the operation as well.

Step 1.5: Measurement Tools for Internal Communications

To get accurate and valid measurement, you need the right tools. The tools we discuss in this section may be used, as appropriate, for both your preliminary benchmark studies in Step 1 and for your data collection in Step 5 below.

Output Measurement Tools and Internal Message Analysis—What you need to understand first, as part of your benchmark study, is whether the output that you are distributing is reaching your internal audience. Are the memos and emails being read? Are they getting to the people and/or departments in a timely manner? Are they being passed along or automatically deleted? Are they reaching the right people?

We refer to this phase of measurement as internal message analysis. We typically analyze all outgoing communications including emails, newsletters, memos, voice mails, videos, speeches, and presentations to determine what messages are being communicated, who is getting the messages, and what they are doing with them, such as deleting them, forwarding them, or saving them for later. More sophisticated clients actually analyze the email traffic to determine connections and networks that are developing. For large organizations, there are systems like Valdis Kreb's *Inflow* (www.orgnet.com) to map the forwarding and response patterns of email.

While most organizations are naturally concerned about over-surveying employees, a quick survey on email usage generally pays off. JPMorgan Chase analyzed email usage and discovered that by managing email communications more efficiently the organization could save several million dollars a year.

Other important metrics are available from your intranet log files: To what extent are people clicking on various pages on your intranet, to what extent are they downloading?

External Message Analysis—Internal communications never functions in a vacuum. Employees are just as likely to get news of company developments from local media or gossip at a soccer game as they are from your emails. Therefore it is critical that you also be monitoring local media to have a complete understanding of what the employee is seeing. For more on media content analysis, refer to Chapters 2 and 3.

Outtake Measurement Tools—This is typically a more in-depth survey that will help you determine what the take-aways are from the messages you are trying to communicate. In other words, did they understand the message, did they interpret it correctly? Did it change their morale, their work habits, and their level of understanding? To what extent did the communications affect their outlook toward the company? We recommend quarterly "pulse checks" of employee attitudes to determine how perceptions are changing over time.

Focus groups can help you probe employees to discover the real issues that concern them and to discover the specifics you want to measure. If the major messages aren't getting through, what is? What are the subtle variations between what the head honchos say and what the employees hear?

Outcome Measurement Tools—Outcomes are the behaviors that you want to affect within your organization. Ideally, your communications efforts are intended to make employees more loyal, more efficient, and more knowledgeable. So the outcome metrics might be employee retention, performance ratings, turnover, or efficiency ratings.

One company developed an ongoing Trivial Pursuit quiz to test employees' knowledge and understanding of the messages. Prizes were awarded for the most right answers. The program significantly increased the entire company's understanding and belief in the key messages.

As with outputs, an important outcome metric is available by studying your intranet's log files. Data such as how long employees spend in each area, to what extent are employees visiting various pages, and the extent to which they download the information you provide are all potentially valuable measures of employee behavior.

Where Do Blogs Fit In?—Increasingly, organizations are using blogs as a way to get messages out to employees and to gather feedback from employees. Companies like Sun and GM rely on blogs to establish two-way conversations with employees and get their messages out. If you have a corporate blog, you have an easy way to track employee responses based not just on the direct comments, but also on the volume of traffic, the number of trackbacks, and the number of other links to the site. See Chapter 10 for how to measure blogs and online relationships.

Survey Details—For surveys to be statistically valid, every employee needs an equal opportunity to participate. In many companies, that precludes email surveys, since not every employee has equal access to computers. In many cases, even phones aren't always within reach. No surprise, then, that so many companies still rely on paper surveys. Although they may be slow and appear antiquated, employees seem remarkably willing to fill them out. Our average response rate for employee paper surveys is around 40 percent.

Phone surveys are a good option for those groups of employees, like managers, for instance, who definitely have phones. We undertook a survey for a major national health concern and found that more than half of the survey population willingly spent 30 minutes with us, discussing the pros and cons of the communications program.

The key, of course, is to ask the right questions. *Make sure that you have a professional researcher craft the survey questionnaire.* It's a deceptively difficult job, and if you get it wrong, you probably won't find out until there's a pile of worthless paper staring you in the face. We often see homegrown benchmarking programs fail because the right questions either were not asked or were asked in a way that failed to yield actionable information. Too many employee attitude surveys measure tactics rather than relationships. Make sure you incorporate the Grunig Relationship Survey questions (see Appendix 1), not just test satisfaction.

Benchmark Study Analysis

After you do the basic benchmark data collection, the information needs to be counted, evaluated, and categorized according to type, effectiveness, messages communicated, and so forth. Examine what messages are being delivered in what formats. You can use something as simple as an Excel spreadsheet, or a more sophisticated database package like KDPaine & Partners' DIY Dashboard (www.diydashboard.com), which gives you a little more flexibility.

Many organizations standardize on cost per message communicated as a way to compare the efficiency and effectiveness of different programs. Another option is to compare the reach and frequency of message communications in various different vehicles, including email, local media, and internal communiqués. You'll probably want to compare and contrast internal versus external communications vehicles to test the degree to which different media outlets and different tactics are successful in communicating your messages.

Step 2: Agree upon Objectives and Messages

Now that you thoroughly understand the environment and your starting point, it is time to get agreement from top management about what you're trying to accomplish. To do this you need to understand the vision, objectives, and messages that senior management wants to communicate.

First, you probably will want to present to key management the information from your benchmark studies (Step 1 above) so that they understand the context. Even if, for timing or other reasons, a formal presentation may not be practical, you or your research partner will want to interview key management and determine what their messages and objectives are. Based on a thorough analysis of your preparatory research, write down very clear, explicit objectives and get senior management to agree to them. What do they think is important? What do they see as the corporate vision? What do they see as the strategic direction? Is the goal of your internal communications program to increase loyalty and productivity? To decrease employee turnover? To help in recruitment efforts? Is the goal to communicate specific messages?

Step 3: Define the Criteria of Success

This process involves defining the actual words and numbers to be used as you create your specific, measurable definitions of success. These criteria are numerical, and most often they are percentages or amounts expressed in dollars or numbers of something. Your definition(s) of success might include, for instance:

- My program will increase understanding of the corporate mission and values by xx percent, or

- My program will decrease employee turnover by xx percent.

This is where you decide what truly defines your success, and where you commit to achieving specific goals. Make sure your goals are achievable.

Step 4: Select a Benchmark to Compare To

Measurement is a comparative tool, and you have to decide what you want to be compared to. It might be last year, last quarter, or another company. The comparison doesn't even have to be with someone in your industry. Telecommunications companies have been known to benchmark against Disney and General Electric because the latter had similar programs.

If possible, find a peer company willing to undergo a similar test. The bottom line consists of comparing your results to something or someone that seems credible to your boss. If you are a telecommunications company and your boss admires Disney, compare yourself to Disney. You and your results will get more respect than if you compare yourself to a company that the boss does not think is important.

It would be nice to be able to compare your results to robust industry-wide statistics, but internal communications measurement is such a young field that few are available. Watson Wyatt Worldwide (www.watsonwyatt.com) does a number of studies of corporate communications that provide general benchmark data such as: Companies that communicate effectively are 4.5 times more likely to report high employee engagement and 20 percent more likely to report lower turnover rates, when compared to firms that communicate less effectively. Their most recent study found that firms within the financial and wholesale/retail trade sectors rank among the most effective communicators, while companies from the basic materials, general services, and healthcare sectors tend to rank among the least effective communicators. Copies of the study are available through www.watsonwyatt.com.

Step 5: Select Measurement Tools and Collect Data

Once you know what you want to measure, the tools that will provide the data and statistics you use to evaluate and compare programs are surveys, and message, traffic, and media analyses. The tools we generally recommend have been discussed in Step 1 above. They're all widely available, and many may already be in place within your organization.

Step 6: Analyze and Take Action

The point of measurement is not just to generate a folder full of charts and graphs. You need to analyze the data, segmenting it across different employee groups to glean insight, draw conclusions, and make recommendations. The idea is to use your hard-won knowledge to improve the effectiveness of what you are doing. Therefore you want to have results in hand when actions can be taken, decisions made, and steps taken toward improvement.

In internal communications, the very act of surveying raises expectations that things will improve or at least change. Getting back to employees is especially important, not just with results but with specific changes that you will make or recommend because of the research.

Step 7: Make Changes and Measure Again

Set up a regular schedule for reporting and planning. "Last week" is generally when most companies need the results of their benchmarking studies. Realistically, you need to work backward from when the results will do the most good. If you do your planning in July and get results in January, the results are six months too late and you're dealing with very old news. Because you don't want a "message du jour," but do want to engender consistency and continuity, we recommend benchmarking every 12 to 18 months.

Chapter 10

Measuring Blogs and Online Relationships

As a general rule the most successful man in life is the man who has the best information.

—Benjamin Disraeli

The Internet has brought about a revolution in marketing far beyond the scope that even the most forward-thinking of us might have imagined. Today, despite the best efforts of PR and marketing types, consumers continue to seize power from the marketers. Mitch Kapor has described the Internet as the "ultimate democratic society—a truly chaotic universe." As *The Cluetrain Manifesto* and *Naked Conversations* so clearly point out, the consumers are the media, the editors, and the reviewers. They are in control and they're going to let you know what they think by changing their behavior.

To paraphrase Ken Kesey, in today's media environment the inmates are now in charge of the asylum. Thanks to advances in technology that have made it incredibly easy and virtually free to create content, consumers, the media, and everyone in between are creating content at unprecedented rates. More and more people—be they journalists, pundits, experts, or ordinary gadflies—are taking to the Internet to put forward their views to anyone who will listen and many are now wielding considerable influence over what consumers buy, think, and do.

**Typical Outputs, Outtakes, and Outcomes
for Measuring Online Relationships**

Outputs: Total opportunities to see (OTS); share of positive OTS; total number of OTS key messages; share of favorable positioning

Outtakes: Percent change in awareness; percent change in preference; percent change in talking about key messages

Outcomes: Percent change in downloads; percent change in sales; percent change in requests for information

Blogs, Social Media, and You

A new blog is created about once every two seconds. New videos are posted to YouTube even more frequently. Virtually everyone with a computer goes online to search for information before making a purchase. Video search is taking over text search as the most popular form of search. Politicians, marketers and individuals are embracing new forms of social networking such as Second Life, Twitter, and Flickr at unprecedented levels.

Most PR people envision the blogosphere as yet another new medium to address, a new way to scream more loudly at their stakeholders. In fact, PR people need to completely rethink their entire approach—from pitching to engaging in "naked conversations." The new reality is, as David Weinberger told the 2007 New Communications Forum gathering in Las Vegas, "There is no market for your message." People now have access to so much content, and have so many ways to gather news and information, that the likelihood of your corporate message penetrating the clutter is virtually nil. Instead, if you engage the audience in a conversation and learn what the social community is looking for and concerned about, you might be able to persuade them to hear your message.

Do Blogs Really Matter?

The quick answer is "Yes." If you care about what your stake-holders are saying, thinking, or doing, you should be paying attention to social media. Even if your audience is limited in size, and bases its decisions on RFPs, specifications, and the personal sales call, there is always a possibility that someone somewhere is having a problem. The thing you need to remember is that when problems occur, you want people to bring them to you, not have private conversations behind your back. Those are the situations that quickly get out of hand.

One major reason to pay attention to what people are saying about you in social media is that most journalists today rely on blogs for story ideas, to check facts, track down rumors, and to investigate scandals. Another reason is that consumers may be discussing your products. If you sell computers, cars, consumer electronics, cell phones, printers, or any number of consumer items that people research or talk about online, you need to pay attention to blogs. If you know that your customers are going online to do research before they decide what to buy, you need to know what those customers are seeing and reading about you.

If you are still up in the air about whether or not blogs are important for you, conduct a quick poll of your audience and find out just how influential the blogosphere is. There's lots of generic research out there, but most organizations would be better off surveying their own customers to find out just how big an impact the blogosphere has. If there is definitely no clear tie between your organization's goals and the blogosphere, then you can relax and go learn about measuring more relevant media.

Does My Company Need to Start a Blog?

First of all, companies don't blog, people blog. Developing a corporate blog is all the rage these days, and for some organizations, like GM and Sun, with CEOs who like to write, have something to say, and are dedicated to blogging, it makes perfect sense. GM and Sun want to get closer to their customers, so their CEOs started blogging as a way to encourage conversations with them. The point is that a blog is a dialog. A blog is not just a corporate website in a different dress. It is not just a marketing tool. It is a way to establish social networks that may help sell products or may not. But direct selling is not the point of a blog.

In order to be effective you have to have something to say. There's a lot of debate as to whether hiring a blogger to ghost write your CEO's blog is ethical. I'm not sure it's unethical; it's just not very effective. The reason blogs become popular is that they reflect the real personalities and values of the people writing them. No one reads a blog to get more corporate speak; they read blogs to get the information *behind* the corporate speak.

Measuring Blogs and Online Relationships

Within this environment, PR researchers need to rethink their approaches. The normal maxim for measurement is, "If you can't measure it, you can't manage it." The problem with measuring blogs is not how to do it, but rather that the nature of blogs renders management impossible. You simply can't manage what 100 million independent-minded, opinionated people are going to say. And woe to those who try; the blogosphere can resemble a cornered porcupine—very prickly—when it senses someone trying to control it.

That's not to say that conversations and relationships on the Internet can't be influenced, just that it takes a new approach for the new environment. The old command and control, top-down message delivery is no longer an option. James Grunig's Excellence Model of two-way synchronous communications (see Appendix 2, Grunig and Grunig, 1992) is the rule of the day. Consumers can now choose to accept or reject your messages, depending on whether they find them useful, interesting, or relevant. And, they'll be more than happy to tell you what they like and don't like.

The biggest challenge to a researcher on the Internet is the sheer enormity of the task. The good news is that technology can help you find your way, and there are a number of organizations out there that will be happy to assist you in gathering your data.

The bad news is that the data you gather will probably have major gaps in it and may be of questionable validity. Organizations like comScore (www.comscore.com) and Neilsen//NetRatings (www.neilsen-netratings.com) are making concerted efforts to audit and verify traffic rates and provide more accurate data on things like page views, hits, and visits. However, there are still gaps. For instance, publications that require subscribers to log on will not be included in most Web searches. Even the most comprehensive search firms can only gather a fraction of what you really want.

Finally, the resources required can be daunting. Remember that for every article that appears in *The New York Times*, there could be 24 that appear in www.nytimes.com—one for every time it updates its pages.

What Do You Want to Measure?

Do you need to measure your own blog, or are you trying to assess what others are saying about you in the blogosphere? The tools and techniques for measuring your own blog are typically financial in nature: assessing ROI, effect on sales, or lead generation.

On the other hand, measuring what consumers are saying about you in their blogs is not all that dissimilar to traditional media analysis in which you are looking at the accumulated content of many blog postings and determining trends and tendencies based on that content. We will address each challenge individually.

Measuring Your Own Blog

As with other forms of communications, before you start trying to measure blogs you need to know what your objectives are. And, as with any other measurement program, there are essentially three things you can measure: outputs, outtakes, and outcomes.

Outcomes: How Does Your Blog Affect Behavior and Relationships?

In the blogosphere, outcomes can be financial, relational, or transactional. If the objective of your blog is financial—to raise money (www.blogforamerica.com) or sell something (www.englishcut.com)—the metrics and the math are very simple. What was the cost per click-through, cost per sale, cost per lead, or the cost per dollar raised?

If the objective is not as directly commercial—for example, you want to move people along the purchase cycle—you can measure the number of people who click through from a blog to your site. The percentage of all visitors who take action or click through is a fundamental measure of success.

Financial Outcomes

More importantly, if you factor in your budget, you will determine your cost per click-through, which can be easily compared to other Web marketing tools. By assigning specific and unique URLs to links, it becomes very easy to track the click-through rate from individual blogs. To determine the efficiency, divide the cost of the program with the number of click-throughs to get cost per click-through.

For example, suppose it costs you $120 a year to set up a blog and you spend an hour a day on it. If you value your time at $150 an hour, your cost for the year is $54,870. If the blog generates 50 click-throughs a day or 18,250 a year, your cost per click is: $54,870/(365 x 50) = $3.00.

Relationship Outcomes

A far more typical desired outcome of a blog, however, is to build relationships with your customers, your employees, or your marketplace. In this case the metrics are quite different. The strength and power of the blogosphere is in the networks it creates and the relationships you can form.

In the traditional marketing space, we would recommend surveying customers to determine their position on relationship components like trust, satisfaction, commitment, and control mutuality. However, the nature of the blogosphere is to eschew traditional marketing techniques in favor of far more direct interactions.

That's not to say that some attempt to measure relationships shouldn't be applied. You could create a mechanism (a contest, free white paper, and so forth) to capture the emails of people who follow your blog and then conduct an email survey using the Grunig Relationship Survey (see Appendix 1).

Traffic Outcomes

At the most basic level, if you are hosting your own blog, the server log files can tell you how many visitors have visited, how long they stayed, and where they came from. Of course the term "visitors" must be taken with a grain of salt, since the technology behind determining a visitor makes very generalized assumptions about human behavior. More sophisticated tools like ClickTracks (www.clicktracks.com), Compete (www.compete.com) WebTrends (www.webtrends.com), WebSideStory (www.websidestory.com), and Omniture (www.omniture.com) provide far more data and, unlike your basic log files, can display it in an understandable way.

Outtakes: Social Capital and Social Networking Measures

Robert Putnam and others have done extensive research on the value of social capital and social networks. In essence, for an individual, the more relationships you have, the better your life is, the longer you live, and the healthier you are. For a company, good social capital means that information flows more easily, innovation and efficiency increase, and legal costs go down. You can extend this concept to the networks created by blogs. If a blog is generating favorable comments, engaging employees or customers in the business of the organization, and disseminating information quickly and accurately, it is contributing to the social capital of your organization.

Outputs: How Many People Are Paying Attention to Your Blog?

Rankings are the currency *du jour* in the blogosphere. The higher you are ranked, the more speaking engagements you get and the more influence you have. Because most rankings are based on the number of links to your site, rankings are a reflection of how important or interesting people find your site. There are a number of sites, such as Technorati (www.technorati.com), BlogLines, and Kineda (www.kineda.com/are-you-an-a-list-bloglebrity), that rank blogs in terms of their popularity. You may want to keep track of your rank over time as a measure of your blog's popularity or influence.

The Conversation Index

Stowe Boyd (www.stoweboyd.com) developed this index as a way to measure the degree to which a blog generates conversations. The conversation index (CI) for a given blog equals the sum of comments plus trackbacks divided by the total number of posts. In general, more comments per blog is better, and a CI of 1 or greater is acceptable. A CI near zero is a pretty good indication that no one cares much for what you have to say, or at least that no one cares to respond to what you have to say.

Simply counting the volume of conversations, comments, and trackbacks is another indication of the size and scope of the network surrounding your blog. Whether or not those comments are in agreement or disagreement requires content analysis, but presumably positive or neutral comments would be indicative of a healthy relationship between the blogger and his or her audience. Again, server log files can tell you how many visitors there have been, how long they stayed, and where they came from.

Measuring Other People's Blogs: What Are They Saying about You?

There's no doubt that a mention in an A-list blog can have both financial and reputational outcomes on your organization; just ask Dell, whose customer service problems were brought to light by a blogger and the resulting outcome was a significant drop in the company's stock price.

More typically, financial outcomes take the form of increased traffic to your website, or increased leads. Reputational outcomes require a longer-term, integrated approach to measurement. First you need to analyze how you are discussed in blogs, and then match the reputational characteristics that are coming out in those discussions with the perceptions that your audiences and stakeholders have of your organization.

Finally, you need to keep close track of the activity to your website and correlate that activity against the various postings in the blogosphere that mention your brand.

Outtakes: What Are Readers Taking Away?

Think of the blogosphere as one enormous focus group with customers, prospects, employees, and potential employees all constantly sharing their thoughts with the world. Content analysis of the blogosphere gives you the opportunity to listen in on their conversations. As a result you should have a much better understanding of how your audiences are responding to your initiatives. However, just reading blogs is not a substitute for a well crafted survey. A survey is better than content analysis for determining what readers have internalized and are taking away from all the chatter.

The words shared in the blogosphere are an important source of outtake information. Content analysis of blogs should look for messages and themes to determine how your customers and constituencies perceive your organization or brand. How does the blogosphere position your brand on issues like employer of choice, value, or customer service? A good analysis will pull out recurring themes, complaints, and messages and quantify them to determine if they require action or can be ignored.

Outputs: Quantity and Quality of the Discussion

While it might give you a good feeling to know that your brand is being mentioned with increasing frequency in the blogosphere, it would be highly dangerous to simply assume this to be good news. Edelman did a lot better when it was one of the least mentioned PR firms in the blogosphere; when it soared to the top of everyone's most talked-about list it was because people were not saying nice things. To determine the quality as well as the quantity of the discussion about your brand requires a thorough content analysis.

Does this mean slogging through 1,000 blogs a day? Probably not. You can generally cut down on the number of relevant blogs by making sure you search only those blogs with high authority. The easiest form of monitoring is to go to Technorati, Bloglines, Sphere, or Google Blog Search and see what people are saying about you. If that seems like too much work, there are several firms that scrape the blogosphere on a daily basis and will send you a daily update based on a selected set of search terms.

One word of caution however; only a small percentage of blog traffic may be of interest to you. The vast majority of conversation is teenage chatter that may or may not be relevant to your stakeholders. While a traditional media feed such as Factiva will deliver about 90 percent relevant content, the opposite is true with social media. Due to the limitations of automated content gathering, typically only about 10 percent will be relevant to the topic at hand.

As with all media old and new, one needs to look beyond just quantity of postings to the quality of the dialog. Postings and comments in blogs can take many different forms. Some may be complaints about customer service, others may be speculation on stock price, and still others may be protests over personnel policies. So the next step in setting up a blog measurement system is to make a list of the various categories the postings fall into and to prioritize the categories. Are they all equally important, or are there some that are potentially more damaging or require faster action?

In the traditional media and in most newsgroups, the vast majority of what is said about a particular organization is neutral. But the unfettered and unfiltered nature of the blogosphere brings more opinions and frequently more negative opinions. Remember to step back as far as you can and remain objective. Think like your target audience. Just because someone leaked a piece of information or got a name wrong is no reason to respond or get involved in a discussion.

Some standard criteria to look for include:

- **Depth of coverage**: The number of times your brand or issue is mentioned within a posting

- **Dominance**: Is the posting exclusively about your brand? Does the blogger go into the subject in-depth with numerous links, or is it just a passing mention?

- **Subject**: The primary topic of the blog posting

- **Tonality**: Did the blog posting leave a reader more or less likely to do business with your organization? Did it make a recommendation or give a specific "don't buy this model" message?

- **Positioning on key issues**: Did the posting discuss any of the key issues facing your industry and if so, how did the blogger position your organization? Did the posting mention any specific benefits that would lead your audience to buy or not buy your product? How was your brand positioned on those benefits relative to the competition?

- **Nature of the posting**: Was the posting designed to solve a problem, compare different brands, or simply allow the author to rant?

- **Who is being discussed or quoted**: Is it your CEO or a minor employee?

Quantifying the Data

There are three essential things that get measured in the blogosphere: links, visitors or eyeballs, and sentiment.

Links and Authority

There are a plethora of services that measure links and rank the importance of various blogs. My particular favorite is Feedster (www.feedster.com), which maintains a ranking of the top 500 most interesting blogs. BlogPulse™ (www.blogpulse.com), BlogLines (www.bloglines.com), and Technorati (www.technorati.com) all rank blogs by the number of links to each blog.

Ever since the first A-list blogger was crowned and Technorati put out its rankings, PR people have been begging for a way to measure authority. The generally accepted practice is to count the number of links, trackbacks, and comments, and roll them up into a ranking or authority index. The simplest thing to do is to look up the URL of the blog on Technorati and see what the rank is (Technorati may not offer rankings in the future). A step up from that is a nifty little Technorati-based widget on the Kineda site that will tell you instantly if a given URL is an A-, B-, C-, or D-list blog (www.kineda.com/?p=1166). There are also a number of businesses who have created products or services around the need for measuring authority.

Another approach is to look at the specific industry and/or market and design an authority index around your particular business or market. This requires more in-depth bespoke research up front, but will yield more useful results in the long term.

Measuring Visitors vs. Eyeballs

As of this writing, there really is no accurate count for the number of eyeballs (which is the same as what we have been calling opportunities to see, or OTS) that view each blog. There are statistics that show the number of visitors and the number of page views, but so far there's no way to exclude the visitors counted every time you or anyone else does a search, so most of those numbers are hugely overstated.

It is safe to say that each link to a blog represents at least one pair of eyeballs. But there is no accurate count of how many people saw the blog posting that included the link. The owner of the blog itself and/or the blog host service has the data, but unless he or she shares it with the public, it remains unknown. For example, you couldn't count the eyeballs reached with a mention in a relatively specialized blog such as the one I operate at KDPaine's Measurement Blog, unless I gave you the analytics that TypePad (the blog provider) gives to me.

The dominant players in the eyeball counting industry for websites are comScore, Compete, Alexa, and Nielsen// NetRatings. They get their data by tracking consumer behavior via software that is loaded onto millions of machines and reports back to the companies exactly where on the Internet those machines have visited. Because there are so many individuals involved in the study, the results are reasonably reliable for the vast majority of websites that they track. Note, however, that just recently some of these numbers have been challenged by the Interactive Advertising Bureau, which would like comScore and Nielsen//NetRatings to submit to a third-party audit of their measurement processes.

While both comScore and Nielsen//NetRatings have started to include a few major blogs (as opposed to websites in general) as part of their panels, and you can sometimes figure out eyeball rates for the major blogs, the vast majority fall into the "too small to count" realm. Because blogs change daily and each new posting takes a reader to a new URL (combined with the fact that there are so many individual blogs and so many links and comments and trackbacks), a panel approach simply won't work because no one is going back to the same page day after day.

comScore has just introduced an engagement metric, based on total visits, average minutes per visit, average visits per visitor, and average visits per usage a day. While it is certainly an improvement over page views, and should help Web properties understand how users are engaging with their content, it appears that the focus of this metric is on websites, not blogs.

Sentiment

Mark Rogers of Market Sentinel (www.marketsentinel.com) has developed a "net promoter's index" that takes the number of bloggers that would recommend your brand, subtracts the number that would not recommend your brand, and comes up with an index number. It's a simple approach, and everyone loves simplicity. I particularly like his recommendation that you look at the index competitively. Rogers claims that there is a direct correlation between the index and sales, and it makes sense. If the number of your detractors outnumbers your promoters, chances are your reputation is being trashed and sales will be affected.

Biz360 (www.biz360.com) just introduced another new metric, Media Signal, that looks at the positive, negative, and neutral coverage in blogs and then factors in the links and connections with an index number to gauge the total impact of a blog.

As far as comments go, measuring them is not even a glimmer in anyone's eye. None of the automated systems track comments, and no one has a clue as to how many people are actually reading comments.

What to Do with the Data Once You Have It

First, take a very deep breath. Do not go into crisis mode the first time you get a negative comment from the blogosphere. Do a bit of research first. Read the blogger's prior postings. See how many links he or she has, how many comments, how many trackbacks. If it's one or two, don't do anything, but watch the numbers. If they start to grow quickly, you may have an emerging crisis. If it's already in the hundreds, and/or if this blog is on the aforementioned Feedster's top 500 list, then you need to come up with a response.

If it's not a crisis, but there is someone who is consistently writing about you, take the wait-and-see attitude. See what kinds of comments are made, and how the blogger responds. Then start a dialog. Offer information, a perspective, or insight on something the blogger will find relevant.

Do not spam bloggers! Generic press releases sent to bloggers will probably get you labeled as a "junk sender" and nothing you ever send will get through. Ever again.

Woe be it to the poor marketer who makes an obvious attempt to manage bloggers or somehow shield their company's reputation. The blogosphere is rife with snide comments and occasional downright hostility toward marketers' blundering attempts to interject themselves into a conversation.

The most important part of any measurement program is teasing insight from the data and drawing actionable conclusions.

The most important analysis is to look at trends over time. What happened yesterday or last week is important, of course, but what you need to do is to see if complaints are going up or down over time, or if your relationships are getting better or worse over time, or if the ranks of complainers are growing faster than the ranks of supporters.

Chapter 11

Measuring Relationships in a Crisis

Great emergencies and crises show us how much greater our vital resources are than we had supposed.
—William James

We only have to look at the response to any of the extreme weather emergencies we've had lately to know that, when it comes to nations and individuals, William James was absolutely right. The veracity of his claim, however, is not nearly as clear cut when it comes to organizations. On the contrary, many corporations in crisis demonstrate just how much *fewer* are their vital resources than previously believed, assuming that vital resources include reputation, leadership, and integrity, as well as customer and employee loyalty. During a crisis all of these factors are put under enormous strain, so the survival of an organization's reputation depends on its internal culture, on the strength of its communications and on the integrity of its leadership.

Before we can examine how to measure how communications affect relationships in a crisis, we need to set down some basic foundations for what constitutes crisis communications. Of course, the best type of crisis communications is that which avoids the crisis altogether. In fact, according to James Grunig, Professor of Public Relations at the University of Maryland (and one of the researchers responsible for the Grunig Relationship

---

**Typical Outputs, Outtakes, and Outcomes
for Measuring Relationships in a Crisis**

Outputs: Volume of negative vs. positive coverage

Outtakes: Percent of people who believe your side of the story

Outcomes: Downloads of explanatories on website; impact on sales and/or market share; impact on relationship scores

---

Survey, see Appendix 1), good crisis communications start way before an incident occurs:

> Communication with publics before decisions are made is most effective in resolving issues and crises because it helps managers to make decisions that are less likely to produce consequences that publics make into issues and crises. If a public relations staff does not communicate with its publics until an issue or crisis occurs, the chance of resolving the conflict is slim.

Grunig articulates four principles of crisis communications:

- **The Relationship Principle**: An organization can withstand both issues and crises better if it has established good, long-term relationships with publics who are at risk from decisions and behaviors of the organization.

- **The Accountability Principle:** An organization should accept responsibility for a crisis even if it was not its fault.

- **The Disclosure Principle:** At the time of a crisis, an organization must disclose all that it knows about the crisis or problem involved. If it does not know what happened, then it must promise full disclosure once it has additional information.

- **The Symmetrical Communication Principle:** At the time of a crisis, an organization must consider the public interest to be at least as important as its own. Public safety, for example, is at least as important as profits. Therefore the organization has no choice other than to engage in true dialogue with publics and to practice socially responsible behavior when a crisis occurs.

To make sure you are doing all you can to avoid a crisis, always listen carefully to your audiences. What issues are surfacing in chat rooms, newsgroups, and in the media? How are employees, vendors, and the community responding to your messages? These questions can easily be answered through regular surveys and media content analysis.

But sometimes all the listening in the world cannot prevent the unavoidable accident, or the simple twist of fate. Through no fault of your own, the TV cameras are at your doorstep and the spotlight is upon you. Your crisis communications plan kicks into effect, your key messages are delivered, the emergency website is live. So assuming that your organization has followed all the rules, how do you know how well you're doing under fire?

The answer is that you measure outputs, outtakes, and outcomes:

- **Measuring outputs and the effectiveness of your process:** Hour-by-hour or day-by-day monitoring of the media to determine if your key messages are being communicated and to whom.

- **Measuring outtakes and impact:** Determining if the messages are being believed and if they're swaying public opinion.

- **Measuring outcomes:** In the long run, did the crisis impact your reputation? Your customers' intent to purchase? Employee turnover? Shareholder confidence?

We will discuss each of these options in this chapter. Which type of measurement you select should be driven by your internal needs for better decision-making tools.

Measuring Outputs: Checking the Volume and Content

A monitoring report typically examines print, television, radio, Internet news groups, and chat rooms to determine what is being said, how the organization is being positioned, and what messages are being delivered.

Daily or hourly monitoring is a wonderful tool, but if you can't respond or react to the data, there's no point in commissioning it. If you are in the midst of a crisis, however, and you need to make decisions hourly or daily as to what to say or not say, such monitoring will be essential. Schedule delivery of these monitoring reports to allow plenty of time to craft and refine the key messages you need to be communicating.

Sometimes the ultimate measure isn't the content, but the sheer volume of crisis coverage. The charts in Figures 11 and 12 track the volume of clips over time for several well-known crises. As you can see, sometimes the volume of coverage goes up after the crisis breaks and sometimes it goes down. That's the difference between well-managed crises and poorly handled ones. A well-managed crisis gets all the bad news over with up front by aggressively dealing with the problem. A poorly handled one can drag on for months.

In the infamous case of the flawed Intel Pentium® chip, Intel long denied the existence of any problem, until finally camera crews showed up on their doorstep. The resulting coverage went on for months.

In sharp contrast, Odwalla, a natural juice company, was found to have sold batches of contaminated unpasteurized apple juice that sickened a number of people and resulted in the death of a child. Its corporate culture, reputation for social responsibility, and crisis communications were so strong, however, that it

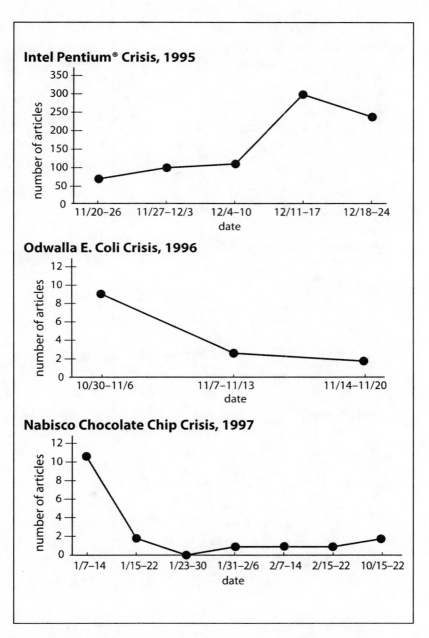

Figure 11. Volume of coverage over time for three crises.

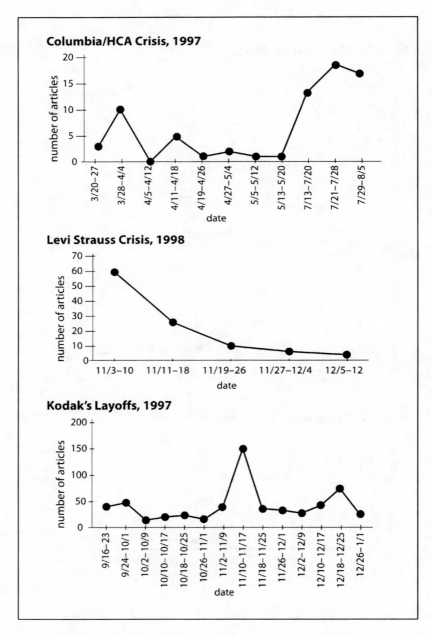

Figure 12. Volume of coverage over time for three crises.

managed to contain the crisis in a few short weeks and ultimately avoided lawsuits altogether.

While Nabisco's story isn't as dramatic, it demonstrates how fast thinking on the part of a member of the public relations team saved the day. An elementary school class released a story saying that Nabisco's Chips Ahoy chocolate chip cookies did not in fact have as many chips per bag as promised. The company immediately sent out a "cookie technician" to the school in North Carolina to help the class repeat the experiment. The new study found more chips than promised and the crisis coverage was gone within a week.

Not so the case of HCA Healthcare, that denied and obfuscated its financial results for so long that the story dragged on for months and eventually lead to the replacement of all top management.

In the case of Levi Strauss's first-ever layoffs, the company took a novel proactive approach by simultaneously announcing grants to all the communities affected. As a result, its coverage spiked the first week, and steadily decreased after that.

Unlike Levi Strauss, Kodak corporation suffered a series of leaks about potential layoffs, eventually announced layoffs, and then had to announce even more layoffs, because the cuts hadn't been deep enough. Again, the result was many, many weeks of bad news.

Measuring Outtakes: Checking Your Messaging

Looking at volume of clips after the fact is one way to judge how effective your actions were, but just getting the messages out into the world is seldom enough to turn around a crisis. Frequently you need to ensure that those messages are being heard and believed as they are going out. The best way to check in with your key audiences in a crisis is through overnight polling. One cost-effective way to conduct overnight polling is to add a question to an omnibus poll. Alternatively, you can commission your own overnight telephone poll, which can cost anywhere from $5,000 to

$25,000. Yes, it's expensive. But, given the cost of talking to your audiences with a full page add in *The New York Times* ($100,000), the cost of listening with an overnight poll seems relatively cheap. And compared to the legal, personnel, and emotional costs of a protracted crisis, research always represents a relatively small percentage.

For example, a major high tech company was under intense pressure at the time of a highly visible sports event, but was able to use a quick poll to ascertain that its key customers were highly supportive of its actions. Despite the ongoing media outcry, the poll data served to calm executives and enabled the company to make more rational decisions.

Measuring Outcomes:
Long-run Effects and Follow-up Research

Post-mortem measurement examines not just how well you did at getting messages communicated, but also demonstrates what ultimate outcomes the program had. Did consumers change their behavior? Did employees leave at a higher than normal rate? Did the stock drop? Did your trust level on Wall Street change? Did your relationships with your employees improve or deteriorate?

Some of these measures are easy, such as looking at the stock price and adjusting for other activity in the market as a whole. Tracking consumer behavior requires broader cooperation with the organization. Frequently, consumer data is readily available from your organization's market research department. There are also many firms that specialize in integrated marketing research. One such firm, Loyalty Builders (www.loyaltybuilders.com) examines customer transactions to determine the impact of events on customer loyalty. It examines how frequently customers purchase, the amount of purchase, and the time between purchases. You can plot that data against your crisis data and look for possible connections.

Even, if you don't have customers you may still need to check on the ultimate impact of a crisis on your target audiences. That's what Habitat for Humanity did after a television reporter in Chicago launched an investigation of its Chicago office. Concerned that the negative publicity might discourage volunteers from participating or donors from giving to the program, it commissioned a survey of target audience members to determine what impact the publicity had on Habitat's reputation. The study showed that, thanks to a coordinated and consistent effort to provide facts, figures and information, and thanks to the fact that the organization had such strong relationships with its constituencies to begin with, the negative publicity achieved scant awareness and had no influence on the audience.

Similar results were found in a research study for a waste disposal company in Texas. The company had sued a television station for libel, charging that a negative story about its dumping of sludge wastes had damaged its reputation. Follow-up survey research discovered that very few people remembered seeing the show and no one remembered the name of the company.

While every crisis differs, follow-up research is critical. No matter what the nature of the crisis or the organization, the best thing that can come of a crisis is learning from your mistakes.

The Seven Steps Applied to Crisis Measurement

Set up your crisis measurement program by following the seven steps outlined in Chapter 1. Work through the first steps below well before you see any crisis coming, because when it does hit, you won't have time to do any careful preparation; you'll be struggling just to keep pace with the events of the day.

Step 1: Define Your Audiences

The first step is to gather in one room managers from public relations, marketing, and employee communications, and anyone else in your organization who can help you define important crisis audiences. List all the possible audiences, including employees, customers, prospects, volunteers, attendees, donors, sponsors, investors or shareholders, the distribution channel, vendors and suppliers, the local constituency, and regulators. Prioritize the audiences and get senior management to agree to those priorities.

This prioritization is important because it determines what publications and media outlets you monitor. For example, if major shareholders are your top priority, you'll want to be particularly concerned about what is being said and heard on Wall Street. However, if you are a small nonpublic business faced with a potential environmental scandal just as plans for your plant expansion are going before the local planning board, tracking what is said in local papers or on the edge of the middle school soccer field might be considerably more important.

Step 2: Define Objectives for Each Audience

Once you've identified and prioritized your audiences, you need to determine how a good relationship with each of those audiences benefits the organization and how a bad relationship might threaten it. It might be that a good relationship does nothing more than prevent lawsuits, or it may be that it results in sales. Either way, you need to articulate what the specific benefits are of your efforts. Because, if in fact the relationship turns bad and the benefits go away, then you need to quantify the failure as well.

Step 3: Define Your Measurement Criteria

Use this list of benefits to create specific criteria against which you can measure your success. Criteria are the hard numbers, complete with time frame, for example, "Communicate key messages in 40 percent of all articles over the next two months," or, "Keep negative messages during the crisis to no more than 10 percent of all coverage."

Step 4: Define Your Benchmark

Who or what are you comparing yourself to? In a crisis, an organization typically measures its own progress over time. It can be significantly more revealing, however, to measure a crisis against some other control group. For example, a study of an airline in crisis looked at its coverage in its hometown paper versus coverage in five other cities. The study revealed that, in contrast to assumptions of the CEO, the local paper actually covered the airline more favorably than papers in other cities, because it tended to provide more in-depth stories, rather than just the negative financials. A similar study compared a company in crisis to other companies in the same town and revealed just how seriously negative the company's coverage actually was.

Step 5: Select a Measurement Tool

We covered crisis measurement tools earlier in this chapter, which will typically be surveys or media analysis. The important point here is to plan ahead and budget accordingly. The general rule of thumb is to allocate 5 to 10 percent of your budget to measurement, but in a crisis, this percentage could be significantly larger, depending on the issues and the complexity of the situation. Remember, good measurement can help you shorten the duration of a crisis, and measurement is cheap compared to the cost of rebuilding your relationships and your reputation.

Step 6: Analyze Results, Glean Insight, and Make Actionable Recommendations

The most important part of the measurement process is to analyze the data and learn from it. What are the actionable points, how can you change and improve? What should you react to? What should you ignore? What needs to be done *today*?

Step 7: Make Changes and Measure Again

Your data-driven insights and recommendations ensure that your measurement system is perceived as worthwhile. Don't be afraid to stand up for them during the crisis and afterwards as well. Your measurement program will become more respected, and you'll be better at it, if you continue the program after the crisis is over. Measurement should always be ongoing and an integral part of your organizational strategy.

Chapter 12

Measuring Relationships Developed Through Speaking Engagements

Give me a fruitful error any time, full of seeds, bursting with its own corrections. You can keep your sterile truth for yourself.
—Vilfredo Pareto

Standing barefoot for half an hour at an airport security checkpoint will make any executive question the value of traveling eight hours in order to speak for 20 minutes. And the lovely meal of cardboard chicken and cheesecake doesn't make the trip any more palatable. So it should come as no surprise that PR professionals are increasingly questioning the value of relationships developed through speaking engagements.

Seven Steps to Measuring Speaking Engagements

To measure speaking engagements, follow the seven steps described in Chapter 1.

Step 1: Specify the Audiences

Who are you trying to reach when you place your speakers? In some cases, it will be sufficient to note that all attendees at a particular conference are your target audience. But other times only a fraction of your speakers' audience is also your target audience. Part of your metrics should include that fraction.

**Typical Outputs, Outtakes, and Outcomes
for Measuring Speaking Engagements**

Outputs: Speaking engagements placed

Outtakes: Percent of audience who heard and believed messages

Outcomes: Change in the number of qualified leads from your booth at the same conference or afterward

---

Step 2: Define Goals and Objectives

Why do you have speakers programs? What are you trying to accomplish? Usually you will answer in terms of awareness of your product or messages, or in terms of time in front of prospects. Answer these questions in terms that you can measure, like, "We want to deliver specific key messages to our target audience." Or, "We want time in front of sales prospects." One way to gain new perspective on your goals is to ask yourself, "What if all our official spokespeople stayed home?" What would then be missing?

Steps 3 and 4: Define your Measurement Criteria and Choose Your Benchmarks

What are your specific, measurable criteria of success, and what will you be comparing those criteria to? Are you comparing the effectiveness of speaker A to speaker B at delivering messages? Are you comparing a trained speaker against an untrained one? Do you want to track your overall speaker program performance over time? The leads or effectiveness of one venue versus another? Set specific objectives, like, "Reached 150 attendees with key messages," or "A majority of people left the conference more likely to try company products."

In terms of relationships, you may want to learn how an audience feels about a particular speaker. Has one speaker in particular, or your program in general, developed or improved rapport or trust with your audience?

Step 5: Pick Your Measurement Tool

The most direct way to measure relationships developed through speaking engagements is to use the Grunig Relationship Survey (see Appendix 1) repeatedly on audiences and note changes over time, between speakers, or between audiences of different media. To compare the nature of your relationships developed through conferences with those developed through experience of other media, use the same questions on both audiences and compare results.

Over the years, we've developed several other metrics for clients that provide some insight into relationships developed through speaking engagements.

Media Analysis of Quotations

Monitor the media coverage around the event to see if your speaker was quoted. If so, determine whether or not the article contained one or more key messages and record the circulation figure of the publication in which he or she was quoted. So if XYZ spokesperson was quoted in *The Wall Street Journal* and the article contained a key message, we would count that as 1.9 million opportunities to see a key message. You can further refine this measure by factoring the visibility of the article, whether it left the buyer more or less likely to purchase the product, and whether the publication was a key publication or peripheral to the program.

Evaluate the Impact with a Questionnaire

If the session organizers allow it, leave a questionnaire on every chair for attendees to fill out. Ask no more than six simple, multiple-choice questions. If possible, use questions from the Grunig Relationship Survey (see Appendix 1) to get a sense of how the speech influenced your relationship. At the very least, determine whether the session attendee heard or believed your key messages and whether they left him or her more or less likely to do business with you. Do this satisfaction survey at the end of each event and you'll get a sense of which events are the best venues for your speakers.

Cost per Minute Spent with Prospect

If you have a product or service that has a long sales cycle and needs time to explain, this is a particularly good way to evaluate marketing efforts. The pharmaceutical companies figure that it costs them $300 to get a salesperson into a doctor's office for about five minutes. That's $60 per minute spent in front of a prospect. Now look at your average speech. You get 60 minutes in front of an audience of 100 people. Say that it cost you $5,000 to get the person there, that's $83 a minute in front of 100 people or $0.83 per minute spent with a prospect. Pretty efficient, when you measure it that way.

You can also use this technique on other marketing efforts. So, for example, if a 20-second underwriting spot on NPR costs $5,000, and assuming it communicates your key message and reaches 500,000 listeners, that's $.01 per opportunity to hear a key message and $0.03 per minute spent with a prospect (assuming that your target audience is NPR listeners—upscale, educated, and so forth).

Cost per Opportunity to See a Key Message

This methodology assumes that one of the objectives for the speakers program is to communicate the company's key messages. In order to calculate the total opportunities to see a key message that your speakers program has generated, attend (or pay someone to attend) all the sessions at which your spokesperson is speaking in order to count the number of people in attendance. Also note the number of targeted versus nontargeted prospects in the session, to provide a more accurate estimate of the audience.

Then review the speech to see which and how many key messages it contains. Multiply that number by the size of the audience and you have the total number of opportunities to see a key message (OTSM). You can then take the budget for the speakers program and divide it by the number of opportunities to see a key message to get a cost per OTSM.

Don't Be Above Using Gimmicks

Calls to action can take many forms, and the best are ones that help you gauge the effectiveness of a program or its ability to develop relationships over the long term. While handouts are pretty much a requirement, it never hurts to offer the audience an additional handout if they give you a business card or go to your website. The best thing about this approach is that you can get a sense from the business card if the lead is qualified or not. In exchange for this added "goodie," you can also ask people to register on your website to determine their location and other details that will tell you whether the speech reached its targeted audience and if it had any impact.

Once they've registered on your website you can then track their purchase behavior through the sales cycle. Keep in mind that for many people it can take six months or longer for them to act on what they might have heard. I recently got a call from a speech I made six years ago. The person was just waiting for the right opportunity to use our services, and a new job provided it.

Step 6: Analyze and Make Recommendations

What decisions are you going to make once you have the data? Don't ask for data you can't use. For example, if you can't fire a spokesperson or promote an alternative spokesperson, then don't measure his or her performance. If you are comparing the suitability of speaking venues, make sure that you have the option to decline an invitation without major repercussions.

Step 7: Make Changes and Measure Again

For any measurement system to work, you need to assess results, make changes, see if those changes had an effect, make more changes, and keep on going through the cycle. Once you begin to understand the relationships created by your speakers, you can begin to revise messages or speeches, better train speakers, or replace speakers in an effort to improve those relationships. You may also want to revisit steps one and two and refine your definitions of your target audiences and objectives.

Chapter 13

Measuring Relationships with Members of Your Organization

When you can measure what you are speaking about, and express it in numbers, you know something about it; but when you cannot measure it, when you cannot express it in numbers, your knowledge is of a meager and unsatisfactory kind.

—Lord Kelvin

Whether your organization's membership consists of 100 civil engineers or 10,000 surgeons, maintaining good relationships with those members and understanding how they view your organization is critical to your success. You can communicate all you want, and get great press, yet still lose membership if your members don't feel they're getting good value for their money. So how do you know just how good your relationship is with your members? You measure it.

Seven Steps to Measuring Relationships with Members

In the past, organizations would use the occasional membership survey to check up on the members. But typically the questions changed from year to year and few organizations could afford rigorous and statistically valid research methods. Today, with standardized survey instruments, inexpensive online survey options, and more efficient ways to reach out to your audiences,

**Typical Outputs, Outtakes, and Outcomes
for Measuring Relationships with Members**

Outputs: Percent of articles containing key messages or positioning statements; percent of articles mentioning the organization; share of coverage of organizational issues

Outtakes: Percent of publics sharing your point of view and/or believing your messages

Outcomes: Percent change in membership, renewals, or dues revenue; legislation passed or stopped

measuring relationships is an option for even the smallest of organizations.

Step 1: Identify and Prioritize Your Audiences

The first step is to understand the characteristics of your various membership audiences, and then prioritize which relationships are most important. Remember that your members are not a homogenous bunch: there are new members, old members, nonrenewing members, former members, and not-yet-members who just need a nudge to get them to send in the form. You need to understand how a good relationship with each group of members can benefit your organization—and how a bad relationship can hurt it. Good relationships with long-standing members of your organization may bring in significant membership dues, but their value may be much greater if that's where your pool of leadership talent resides.

Similarly, new members have value far beyond their dues, since they may help spread the word, be the most active volunteers, or become attendees at new events. So make a list of all your constituencies, and next to each one list the benefits that a great relationship with that group would bring to your organization.

Then gather senior management and key communications people within your organization and get them to prioritize the audiences. Put all the names up on a chart, and give everyone 10 colored dots. Each dot is worth, say, $100,000 of communications budget (just think of it as Monopoly money). Ask all participants to "spend" their budgets by sticking their dots up next to the audiences they think most important. The audiences with the most dots are clearly the highest priority.

Step 2: Define Your Objectives

The most important thing to remember about any measurement program is that you become what you measure. Those metrics that you define as important will be the ones that everyone in communications will attempt to achieve, so getting them right at the start is crucial. To help define objectives, one exercise we put our clients through is to have them complete a questionnaire that includes the following questions:

- What data do you need to make better decisions in your job?

- Suppose you were so successful that your boss gave you a 20 percent raise, a case of champagne, and an extra week off. What kind of achievement would prompt such a reward? What would then be different in your department and your organization?

- List the target publics that your organization relates to, including both those that threaten and those that benefit your organization.

- Now, for each of those publics, list how a good relationship can benefit your organization.

Look at the list of the benefits a good relationship brings to the organization and see if any of them will translate into measurable objectives. For example, if your organization's number one priority is to grow, then "communications cost per new member added" might be a key metric. If your mission is to enact or defeat legislation, the metric might be "number of bills passed," or some measure of the degree to which your point of view is communicated in the media. If you're trying to engage people or sell product from your website, you might want to make some measure of Web traffic a key metric.

Step 3: Understand Where They're Coming From

When you're thinking about metrics, remember that audiences do not live in a vacuum, nor do they hear only your messages. In today's society any one of your members is hit with some 5,000 messages a day from a wide variety of sources. Some, such as advertising and direct mail, you can control. Others, like the media, you can't. A good measurement program looks at as many different influences as the budget allows. At the very least take into account what your members are seeing in the media, what they're exposed to online, what they're hearing from you, what they're taking away in terms of impressions, awareness, or understanding, and ultimately what actions do they take—renew membership, get friends to join, volunteer, and so on. All these various influences on members affect your relationship with them. So it's necessary to understand and quantify those influences if you want to understand why the relationship is improving or deteriorating.

Step 4: Establish a Benchmark

If I tell you that 35 percent of your members think your organization is the best thing that ever happened to them, you don't know if that's good or bad. It could be bad that 65 percent of the audience *doesn't* feel that way. But on the other hand, if only 15 percent of them thought a competing organization was worth joining, then 35 percent looks like a great number.

Measurement is a comparative tool, so benchmark your results against someone. It could be a peer organization or a competitive organization. Unlike in corporate America, cooperation between nonprofit organizations is common, and organizations can partner on the research in order to have something to compare their results to. Whether you select competing organizations or peer organizations, try to limit the number of entities in any given study to no more than five. Three is ideal, anything more than five becomes unwieldy.

Step 5: Pick a Measurement Tool

Once you have your objectives clear and your benchmarks established, you can decide whether you're going to be measuring outputs (articles that appear in the media); outtakes (what people are thinking as a result of those articles), or outcomes (what people are doing as a result of those articles). Depending on what you're measuring, you will need to analyze your media coverage or survey your membership—preferably both. See Chapter 2 for more on measurement tools and costs.

Measuring Outputs

You don't have to analyze the world, just those publications or media sources that are most important to your audience. Once you've established a key publication list, make sure you have access to all articles in those media outlets, either via your own subscriptions or via clipping services like Bacons, Burrelle's, Factiva, LexisNexis, Cyberalert or CustomScoop.

Every article should be read for the following criteria:

- The main subject

- The type of article it is: opinion, feature story, Q & A, letter to the editor, and so on.

- The visibility of the organization within the article: Was your organization the focal point, or did it just receive a minor mention?

- Who, if anyone, was quoted in the article and what was his or her affiliation?

- The tonality: Did it leave the reader more or less likely to join your organization?

- The type of media in which the article appeared: TV, magazine, business press, and so on.

- Which, if any, key messages were communicated?

- How was the organization (and its peers) positioned on key issues such as "good value for the money," "effective advocate for the industry," or "responsiveness?"

If you don't hire an outside firm to conduct this research, there are several software programs out there that make it a lot easier, including KDPaine & Partners' own DIY Dashboard (www.diydashboard.com).

Measuring Outtakes

To measure outtakes you need to do a survey. The Grunig Relationship Survey can be used with a high degree of accuracy to judge the health of your relationships and their underlying components (see Appendix 1). It provides great insight into how your members view your relationship and organization. You don't need to ask every question, but make sure you test every element of the relationship—trust, commitment, satisfaction, and so on.

These questions can be administered in person, by telephone, or by email. In person will probably get the most accurate responses, but can be very time consuming and therefore the most expensive alternative. Phone surveys are probably the best way to get a sufficient quantity of reliable data, but they, too, can be expensive. Online surveys by companies like SurveyMonkey and Zoomerang are available for essentially free. The trick is to make sure you have a good email list of your members.

Measuring Outcomes

Member behavior can take many forms: renewals, donations, Web traffic, email responses, phone calls, attendance at trade shows, votes, etc. All are relatively easy to measure, once you have a tracking system in place. The key is to keep track of them on a monthly basis, and then compare the results to your media activity and ideally to the attitude research. With sufficient data you will be able to see correlations between activities in the media, communications with your membership, and behavioral outcomes.

Step 6: Analyze the Data and Glean Insight

All the data in the world is simply trivia if you can't draw conclusions from it. So when the data is in, look for trends over time and for differences between groups, like new members versus old members, males versus females. By all means, look most carefully at the bad news and the failures, because that is where you will learn the most.

Step 7: Make Changes and Measure Again

Once you have your member relationship measurement program in place, make it a regular, ongoing part of your communications process. When the data comes in, learn from your successes and mistakes, make changes, and then see the results in the next reporting period. One caveat: Make sure the data is available when you need it. If you do all your budgeting and planning in August, having data at the end of the calendar year does you no good whatsoever. Or if you know you are going to be writing a big grant application, plan your research so you have the data available just before you write it. The data and analysis should be fresh just as you need it.

Chapter 14

Measuring Relationships with Sales People, Channel Partners, and Franchisees

Far more crucial than what we know or do not know is what we do not want to know. One often obtains a clue to a person's nature by discovering the reasons for his or her imperviousness to certain impressions.

—Eric Hoffer

If marketing is from Venus and management is from Mars (see the introduction to the Glossary), sales people are from a different solar system altogether. Whether they're your own internal sales force, franchisees, or channel partners, they are very distinctly "other," isolated either by geography, legal standing, or responsibility. Unlike PR people, who spend most of their waking hours worrying about the media or their internal clients, sales people spend all their waking hours, and most of their sleeping ones as well, worrying about the customer.

Over the years, as we have developed several ways of measuring relationships with salespeople, we have had to take into account their very different perspective. First of all, you can expect their attitude to be: "I'm expected to spend my time selling, but the home office deluges me with new products and new information that I'm supposed to find time to read and talk about with the clients. And then, of course, the really important stuff the home office never tells you about; you have to find that out from the local papers, the customers or, worse yet, the competition."

**Typical Outputs, Outtakes, and Outcomes
for Measuring Channel Partners and Franchisees**

Outputs: Percent change in volume of traffic to Intranet

Outtakes: Percent of employees agreeing with the messages that are being communicated in the media and vice versa (not satisfaction, but agreement and belief in messages)

Outcomes: Percent change in salespeople selling range of products; percent change in sales and/or market share; percent change in salespeople meeting goals

---

Yes, we have heard of at least one salesperson who actually got their company's new and unannounced product price list from his competitors, not his own office.

Millions Spent on Sales Communications, but Does Any of It Work?

I used to be the home office person sending out all that information. I spent millions of dollars each year in writing, designing, and producing pieces of paper that were supposed to make my sales force more effective. Whether it ever worked or not was never questioned—it was just what we did. Today, fortunately, most of the wanton production of breast-beating brochures has been replaced by equally hyperbolic websites—less wasteful of forest products, but no less time consuming to produce and manage.

And in fact, very few organizations know whether any of it is effective. A major computer manufacturer I recently worked with took a long look at its entire communication process, queried its sales force and reduced the number of information sources from 50 to four. For real emergency news it now uses voice mail. For urgent communications, there's a broadcast email. For background information, it relies on an internal website and for broad-based strategic announcements it uses video conferencing.

Questions still remained, however, about the usefulness of those sources. I helped the company design a research project that not only would determine whether the sales force liked the new approach, but also would correlate the flow of information against specific sales performance. Here's how it worked.

Just as the new communications strategy was being announced, we conducted a benchmark survey of the sales force. The study queried individual sales people on their awareness and usage of the various communications vehicles, and their understanding of the messages that the home office was trying to convey.

After six months of communicating via the new system, we again asked the sales force about their awareness of the various vehicles and their understanding of the key messages. What was particularly exciting about this project was that we also knew who was selling what, how much, and how often. So in addition to measuring overall satisfaction with the program, we used a secondary analysis to see if it was translating into actual sales. Using a list of the top 25 sales people, we compared their sales performance, their survey responses, and the degree to which they used the new tools. The analysis showed that heavy users of the new online tools were more likely to be effective sales people.

The Problem: Mixed Messages, Mixed Objectives

Another element of measuring relationships with sales people is what happens if you don't have a direct sales force and/or have little control over the communications processes. For example, if you're providing materials to franchisees or other channel partners. Any corporation that uses franchising as a way to distribute its product or service faces a dilemma unknown to its counterparts in other industries: How to maintain an overall consistent corporate image while allowing franchisees the freedom to develop programs that are customized to their local audiences?

In some ways, this problem strongly resembles what many U.S. companies face in expanding their communications efforts overseas. They need localized communications support, while participating in an increasingly global community where they must maintain a consistent worldwide image. Balancing these two needs is difficult enough, but measuring the effectiveness of these types of programs can be even more so.

One challenge arises from the mix of objectives. For example, one of the most frequently mentioned goals we hear is, "To reach our target audience with our key quality message." This goal is great as long as the target audiences are the same. But what if one franchisee targets seniors and the next targets college students?

Another difficulty involves the mix of activities that franchisees can get involved with. What if one market has just undergone a natural disaster (all too common in the past few years) and the franchisee in that area is able to respond with a particularly effective relief effort? How will that impact a measurement program?

A third problem consists of getting buy-in from the huge cross-section of entrepreneurs who own the franchises. Notoriously independent, entrepreneurs stay up at night for radically different reasons than those that keep a typical corporate communications person awake. Franchisees worry about profitability, staffing, and on-time deliveries. They not only worry about what the bank and their customers think, but also about the consistency of their key messages, their budgets, and the opinions of the boss and the press.

The Solution: Consistent Messages

The key to an effective program lies in finding some common ground among all these different communities. That common ground must be a set of common objectives—not as difficult to find as you'd think. Consistency in advertising messages is a given, that's why national advertising campaigns exist. The challenge in PR is that you don't have as much control over what messages are being really communicated. And without a measurement program, you have even less. By quantifying what the media are saying about you and who is seeing those messages, some control over the image begins to be established—and at a far lower cost than a national advertising campaign.

So one objective that both the corporation and the franchisee can agree on is the need for consistent communication of a few nationwide corporate key messages. This supports the advertising program and makes everyone's dollars go further. If you have a good relationship, the franchisee follows the guidelines you set and is consistent in their branding and their communications. If you have a bad relationship, it'll go its own way and introduce inconsistency in your branding efforts.

The criterion for success then becomes the percentage of articles that contain your key messages. This is determined by having an independent reader (not a PR person or a franchisee) analyze the media to determine what he or she takes away from each article.

Other Measures of Success: More Visibility than the Competition

It is critical that your publicity programs break through the clutter and get your name out in more prominence than that of the competition. This doesn't just mean more articles. It means more mentions of the company or corporation name in headlines, captions, or other places of greater visibility.

The criterion for success in this case could be sheer volume of coverage compared to the competition. An even better qualitative measure would be percent of articles featuring the company name in the headline. This figure then is compared to the percent of articles that mention the competition's name in the headlines.

Better Image than the Competition

Since a major focus of any local promotional program is community good will, you can analyze media coverage to determine how effectively local publicity programs generate that goodwill (see Chapter 8). The most direct means to measure this could be by phone or intercept surveys of the local population. However, since that can quickly become prohibitively expensive, analyzing media coverage again becomes a cost-effective alternative.

As part of the analysis, the reader should note the number of articles that portray the company or brand as a "responsible corporate citizen." Since the competition, no doubt, is conducting similar programs, the reader should also look for the number of articles discussing other brands or companies as good corporate citizens.

Getting Visibility for Local Franchisees

Another element of a publicity program involves establishing company spokespeople as community leaders or reliable sources on topics of interest. This ensures opportunities for franchisees to increase their visibility in the local media. Obviously if your spokesperson gets quoted more often than the owner of a competitive franchise, your program is more effective. It is critical, however, that spokespeople communicate the key corporate messages during these interviews. By tracking not just who is being quoted, but what is being said, you can develop a very effective tool for improving your community relations. If the local folks are on message, then it implies that the local and national offices have a good relationship.

Case Study: Blue Cross Blue Shield Cures Their Image Problem

Blue Cross Blue Shield is a good example of a strong national brand that is carried and promoted by very independent and diverse franchisees. We worked with one franchisee, Blue Cross Blue Shield of New Hampshire (BCBS-NH), to establish a benchmark for its communications efforts, conducting a competitive analysis of the company's public relations and public perceptions. Analyzing all press coverage for BCBS-NH and its two key competitors, we then interviewed two market segments, business decision makers and individual subscribers. We wanted to find out what issues were most important to them, where they got their information regarding health care, and what their current perceptions were of various companies.

Our findings revealed some serious problems in the company's overall image. Based on that information, BCBS-NH revamped its entire communications strategy and crafted new key messages that resulted in a significant turnaround for the company.

At the same time, the national Blue Cross Blue Shield Association was also reviewing its image and rolling out a new theme in a major new advertising campaign. Blue Cross Blue Shield of New Hampshire leveraged this increased national exposure by incorporating the national key messages into its own campaign. BCBS-NH's new awareness of potential subscribers' specific concerns enabled it to adjust key messages to clearly address those concerns while distinguishing itself from the competition. Because the research was already in hand, it was able to quickly develop a complementary strategy that played off the national theme and responded to the needs and perceptions of the local audience, thereby increasing its local visibility.

Chapter 15

Measuring Relationships with the Investment Community

A true measure of your worth includes all the benefits others have gained from your successes.

—Cullen Hightower

For years, measuring relationships with investors was deemed unnecessary since the only metric that really mattered in the investor relations world was stock price. Essentially, everyone assumed that if IR was done right, the stock price would reflect the quality of the effort.

But somewhere between the dotcom bubble and the Quest collapse all that changed. In some ways, Federal Reserve Board chairman Alan Greenspan's comments about "irrational exuberance" summed it up nicely. Essentially, the market stopped behaving in a way that people could predict. Companies that had no product, no profit, and no foreseeable future were suddenly worth a fortune. Startups were worth more than companies that had been around for a hundred years, and individual investors entered the market in record numbers.

IR professionals as well as their colleagues in corporate communications began to see a connection between their efforts and the movement of a company's stock. They began to practice some of the same measurement techniques, including surveying their colleagues to test the health of their relationships, monitoring

**Typical Outputs, Outtakes, and Outcomes
for Measuring Relationships with Shareholders**

Outputs: Share of coverage in financial press

Outtakes: Share of favorable quotes by analysts (what they believe)

Outcomes: Change in stock price; change in share of coverage in analysts' reports;
change in volatility

media coverage competitively, and examining analyst coverage
to determine the success of their efforts.

Measuring Relationships with Individual Investors

For years, most companies essentially ignored individual investors, figuring that to communicate with individuals was not worth
the effort, since most of the influence on stock price came from
institutional investors. However, recent research reveals that companies ignore the individual investor at their peril. First of all,
you can't argue with the numbers. Half of all Americans today
own stock, up from 32 percent in 1989, and the predictions are
that by 2010, 85 percent of Americans will own stock, signaling
an enormous change in the nature and character of investors.

With that in mind, Ernie Martin of Virginia Commonwealth
University set out to explore the impact of PR on investor relations
and presented his findings at the 8th Annual International Public
Relations Research Conference. Looking at specific companies,
he used Elliot Wave Theory to examine what type of investors
were investing in a company at any given time. He found that
when individual investors were involved, stocks stayed up longer
and recovered faster from slumps. He further investigated the
press coverage of the same companies during the periods when
individual investors were getting on board, and found that those

companies that had aggressive PR programs and high media visibility were more likely to attract individual investors and thus saw greater stock volume. More interesting was that those companies that had no major press effort had fewer individual investors and tended to take longer to recover from slumps.

The challenge, of course, is to determine exactly what kind of relationship you have with the investing masses out there. Typically, a company starts with a basic analysis of the business and investor media to determine what the individual investors are seeing. This is frequently supplemented by a review of existing reputation studies such as *Fortune*'s Most Admired list and *Fast Company*'s Top 100 list. Omnibus surveys are also a cost-effective way to determine how the public perceives your company's value. GfK's NewsFlow® offers a cost-effective way to gauge your reputation for less than $4,000 per year.

Measuring Relationships with Institutional Investors

The following five steps are somewhat different from those outlined in Chapter One.

Step 1: Outputs—What Are They Reading About You?

The first step in any institutional investor measurement program is to determine what those investors are seeing about you. You need to make sure that your media analysis program can or will incorporate the key analyst reports. You need to track not just the number of analyst reports written about the company but also the quality of that coverage. Are the reports accurate? Who is writing them, key or fringe players? Do they reflect your messages and strategies?

Step 2: Outtakes—What Are They Saying About You?

You also need to make sure that your media analysis program is tracking the quotes from Wall Street brokers. Monitoring what the firms are saying provides a critical barometer of the general word on the street. To get started, turn to your existing database, spreadsheet, or analysis module to record the name of the publication, the name of the reporter, and to list everyone quoted in stories about you, your industry, or your competition. This will give you a list of most frequently quoted sources.

You now need to record several other details about the article: Was it entirely about you or your industry or category? Did the influencer quoted refer directly to your organization, or was the quote about someone else? And finally, did the article and/or quote contain one or more of your key messages?

Step 3: More Outtakes—What Do They Think About You?

While it is useful to know what they're saying in print, monitoring media will not yield sufficient data and should be supplemented by an annual survey evaluation of your overall relationship with key Wall Street influencers. You can use many of the same techniques that you use in journalist audits, including the Grunig Relationship Survey (see Appendix 1), to survey securities analysts, portfolio managers, stockbrokers, individual investors, and the financial media. Conduct these studies by phone or email, and ask the influencers about their understanding of your organization. Specifically, probe the extent to which they understand your strategies and mission, the extent to which they believe in management's ability, and their overall image of, and trust in, your organization.

Further goals of the survey should be to determine:

- Level of awareness of the company
- Knowledge of corporate strategy and positioning
- Evaluation of the company on specific reputation attributes such as trustworthiness, transparency, solid management.
- Likelihood to hold or recommend stock

With opinion leaders it is particularly important to compare your organization to your peers and competitors, so make sure you ask them how your organization ranks in their minds relative to others in the industry.

Step 4: Outcomes—Success Is a Fair Value for Your Stock

To simply say that success can be measured by an increasing stock price is not a realistic goal. Stock price can be affected by everything from natural disasters to rumors. The right metric is a fair market value of the stock. Other possible metrics include P/E ratio relative to your peer companies, and volume of trades (most companies want a stable trading volume).

Step 5: What to Do with the Data Once You Have It

Tracking analysts can also help identify new opportunities for influence. At one time, my firm was tracking a core list of critical analysts for a major computer company. As it turned out, some of the members of that list were seldom quoted, and sometimes new names would appear. By providing the client a regular update of new influencers each month, we were able to continuously improve the effectiveness of the analyst relations effort. Ultimately we were able to show that this effort nearly doubled the percentage of articles containing key messages over the prior year.

Other issues that should be considered when data from IR measurement is available are:

- Is the level of awareness appropriate to the standing of the company in the marketplace?

- Is there broad and accurate awareness of the company's positioning or are there issues that need to be corrected?

- What element of the program is the weakest and how can it be addressed?

- What moves are the competition making that need to be addressed in future communiqués?

- How solid are the current recommenders of the stock? Are there vulnerabilities among specific analysts that need to be addressed?

Chapter 16

Putting It All Together in a Dashboard

If you go to work on your goals, your goals will go to work on you. If you go to work on your plan, your plan will go to work on you. Whatever good things we build end up building us.
—Jim Rohn

The term "dashboard" began to surface in corporate America about a decade ago when harried CEOs decided that the problem was not a lack of information, but rather too much information. They wanted to define specific gauges that would provide information on whether their organizations were headed in the right direction. The idea was that, like the dashboard in a car, their organizational dashboard would have warning lights to indicate what areas they needed to pay attention to, regular financial reporting so they could quickly tell whether they had enough fuel or resources to get where they were going, and specific gauges for different departments so they could know instantly which areas were performing well and which were performing poorly.

The first gauges to populate CEO's dashboards came from sales and manufacturing and featured metrics like revenue per employee, percentage of contract wins, and sales versus goals. Soon customer satisfaction and loyalty scores were finding their way onto dashboards and inevitably the spotlight came around to communication. Indices like share of discussion, favorability ratings and impact scores began to show up on communications dashboards throughout corporate America, driven in part by new tools like Cymfony's Brand Dashboard™ and Biz360's Market360™ that could provide dashboard-like data at your fingertips.

Five Steps to Create Your Own Dashboard

In these more accountable times, companies are increasingly looking to integrate those media metrics with other performance data to show the true impact of the efforts of an entire communications program. In this chapter you'll learn how to create your own dashboard in five steps, loosely based on the seven steps described in Chapter 1.

Step 1: Make Sure You Know What They're Paying You to Do

The first step in creating your dashboard is to define exactly what it is that the organization expects from corporate communications. The answer is not going to come from within your department. You need executive or board level definitions of what it is they expect you to do. The answer is not always an easy one to get out of them, so it's important to ask the question in the right way.

Essentially, the question is: If you wiped out the corporate communications department entirely, what would happen? What aspect of the business would suffer? It's not enough to say that, "We'd get less publicity." Ask "So what?" So what if our customers have less chance to read about us, and more opportunities to see news about the competition? Does it affect our market share? Our share price? Our profitability? Our credibility? If we have no one to manage our relationship with the local community, so what? Does that mean longer lead times when we want to expand because opposition groups are more hostile? Does it mean that we have a harder time attracting and keeping talent? By assuming the absence of a corporate communications department and understanding the potential consequences, you quickly understand the role that you are expected to play.

Step 2: Define to Whom You Are Relating

Once you've defined the fundamental role that corporate communications is expected to play in the organization, it is equally important to define exactly which audiences and which relationships you are managing. So gather together as many communicators as possible in one room and brainstorm about which audiences and which audience segments are important—the more, the merrier. Do a frank and honest assessment of all the people you currently do talk to, as well as the ones that you *should* be talking to. List them all in one column, and to the right, write down how a good relationship with that audience benefits your organization.

Obviously you can't measure relationships with every audience at once, so your next step is to decide which audiences you are going to measure first. The way to make this decision is to look at the benefits in the right hand column and force rank the audiences based on those benefits. You increase buy-in to your entire project by getting everyone involved to participate, so make sure that all the important decisionmakers and their departments that will see your data are part of the ranking process.

Step 3: Determine Your Benchmarks

Decide what you're benchmarking against. Ideally, it will be your most direct competition or whomever your boss perceives as your competition. And if you are a nonprofit organization and you are thinking, "I have no competition," think again. You are definitely competing for a share of the philanthropy wallet whether you want to admit it or not. So team up with your fellow nonprofits to do a benchmark study of nonprofits in your community. By sharing costs and data you'll be able to get much more data for your dollar, and you'll learn things that you could never hope to uncover if you were only looking at your own data.

Don't make the universe too broad. Realistically you can analyze, keep track of, and manage only about three competitors, as well as yourself. So think in terms of choosing a peer organization, a stretch goal, and an underdog who is nipping at your heels.

Step 4: Undertake the Research

There are always at least three different components to your research:

Output Tracking

First you need to know what your audiences are seeing about you, otherwise you are measuring in a vacuum. Collect data from all your audiences' sources. Ideally, you will have media data from your ad agency that will point to which media are the most influential. Absent such data, you might want to conduct your own research to find out which sources your audiences are using and find most credible. Sources must include all forms of media that offer your constituencies an opportunity to see your messages: Discussion groups, websites, underwriting and sponsorships, employee publications, print, and broadcast.

You also have to make sure that the media you are tracking does in fact reach your desired constituency. For that you need to analyze the demographic and psychographic reach of the publications in which your audiences' articles appeared. Advertising agencies or media departments typically have this information available. If not, comScore and PRTrak have good databases of circulation figures, which will at least give you the raw numbers in a consistent manner.

Once you have the right media, collect articles and analyze them to determine if they do in fact contain your key messages.

You need to see how you are positioned vis-à-vis the competition. You should note who is quoted to determine your share of visibility and influence on your audience.

Outtake Measurement

Once you are sure that your messages and information are actually getting in front of your audiences, you need to determine if your audiences did in fact receive the information. Do they remember seeing the message? Do they believe it? Is it relevant? In other words, have you broken through the clutter and made an impact on them?

There is only one way to get this information and that is to use a survey to ask them. Whether you conduct a survey online, in person, or by phone, you need to determine with some degree of confidence that your messages have in fact reached the audience. As mentioned earlier, GfK (www.gfk.com) has a nifty little product called NewsFlow,® which offers a very reasonably priced omnibus survey that can provide such data.

Outcome Measurement

The next component of the research is to determine whether in fact your audiences were motivated to act by your messages. To do this, look outside of the communications department and assemble the data necessary to track your audiences' behavior after they've seen, heard, and believed your messages. The behavioral data may come from tracking Web visits, downloads, registrations, or sales. Alternatively, it may be available from your human resources, sales, customer service, or finance department.

The key element to your success here is to break out of your silo and realize that by integrating your data into that from other sources, the story becomes much more powerful and useful to your organization as a whole. Go back to your priority chart and look at the behaviors and benefits you listed there. Approach the appropriate sources in your organization that will have access to data concerning them. Don't forget data that may be in public records, such as the Congressional Record or attendee figures at public events.

Case Study: A Private School Wants to Learn the Right Lessons

A private school recently requested that my measurement firm conduct a dashboard development session so that it could develop metrics and measure the effectiveness of each of the departments in its community relations and communications group. The idea was to figure out the extent to which their activities were supporting the organization's goals, as well as where they needed to focus in the future. The nine departments included:

- Technical outreach (including the website)
- Media management
- Design and production
- Communications services
- Brand management
- Internal communications
- Advertising
- Government relations
- Community relations

The organization as a whole had very clearly stated goals and each group had specific goals that tied into the overall organizational goals. We worked with each group individually to develop specific metrics that would be both meaningful and manageable for the group. Once we designed the metrics, we developed custom templates for each group to record the pertinent data. They were required to record the costs for a project and to select one of the corporate objectives that each project supported.

With that data in hand, the school decided that their overall department metrics should be:

- Cost per target audience reached
- Cost per key message communicated to target audience
- Overall key message communication to target audience
- Total outreach to target audience by department
- Percent of target audience hearing key messages
- Percent of target audience believing key messages

What made the program especially useful is that it enabled the department as a whole to look at each project and each effort it was undertaking to see how it contributed to the overall corporate goals as well as the department's goals.

Where to Get the Data

The easiest way to get the data is to walk down the hall and ask someone else in your organization for it. Chances are pretty good that somewhere in your organization someone is tracking customer behavior, customer resource, customer satisfaction, donations, applications, or some other business impact that you have listed in that right hand column in your priority chart.

If your organization has no such data, your task is a bit more difficult but far from impossible. If you are a nonprofit, chances are that someone on your board of directors may have some research capabilities you can tap into, or you can use volunteers, universities, or other research organizations to acquire the data. If worse comes to worst, you can actually go out there and buy it. Roper, Milward Brown, Echo Research, Taylor Nelson Sofres, and many others do a great job providing in-depth integrated marketing research that can track your products' performance against a variety of different factors, including corporate communications efforts.

Step 5: Turning Data into Action

Accumulating the data is only a small part of the overall integrated research process. Making it meaningful is where the "Ah Ha!" moments begin to happen.

First of all, make sure the data is on hand when you're ready to make decisions. That means you need to have it handy at budget season, and pretty much whenever you are asked to make a decision about what money to spend on which project. That may be weekly, monthly, or quarterly, depending on your organization, but the point is that the dashboard should be available and current when the data is needed, not according to any other arbitrary timetables.

Further, it's important to draw the correct conclusions from the data, which is why it is so critical to look at all three data points—output, outtake, and outcome—in an integrated fashion. It's great that you created a million opportunities to see and that everyone remembered seeing those messages, but if it didn't increase sales or market share, there could be something seriously wrong with your message. Alternatively you can identify areas of missed opportunity by examining the three data points as an integrated whole. If discussion and downloads for a particular brand or product line are soaring among the early adopters on your website, this might be an excellent time to roll out a broader communications program via print and broadcast.

The good news is that once you're out of your silo, you'll find lots of other data that can help you. Most market research groups and product marketing departments have historical data. Use it to look at trends in behavior and sentiment and compare them to the trends in your media content analysis. If you don't have a research group, contact your local university or college with a research department and it may be able to provide you with an intern to help.

Case Study: A Major Travel Services Company Needs a Road Map

The new head of corporate communications for a major travel services company came to my measurement firm with a very clear charter: Come up with metrics that will measure the effect of her division and make sure they tie back to corporate objectives. Her division included media relations, events, customer relations, and internal communications. Getting a common metric would not be easy, given the diverse agendas of each department head. Nonetheless we conducted a dashboard development session with the entire team and came up with clear definitions of success for each group:

- For **events**, the driver was cost per target or prospect reach. The events budget was being reduced significantly, but the department still needed to reach just as many, if not more, qualified prospects. Another key factor for the events department was the amount of face time it won with at-risk customers and highly qualified prospects. We decided on cost per minute spent with prospect as a metric.

- For **media relations**, the metrics were relatively simple. We would analyze articles about the company and calculate share of discussion, share of quotes, share of positive positioning on key issues relative to the company's key competitors, and number of key messages.

- Virtually all **internal communications** efforts were via email, with the exception of a few major training sessions. Each email was reviewed to see who it was targeted to and if it contained a key message.

- **Customer relations** communicated major developments to customers using a variety of efforts from email to brochures. Once again we looked at key messaging as a common goal. We took into account the cost of various projects and whom they reached to calculate cost per message communicated.

After we achieved consensus on the individual department metrics, it was relatively simple to define the overall corporate communication metrics as:

- Cost per message communicated

- Cost per contact reached

- Total communication of key messages by department

- Cost per minute spent with target customer

For costs we used the total budget for the entire corporate communications group for the quarter we were measuring.

Epilogue:
Whither Measurement?

The best way to predict the future is to invent it.
—Alan Kay

The future of public relations lies in the development of relationships, and the future of measurement lies in the accurate analysis of those relationships. Counting impressions will become increasingly irrelevant while measuring relationships and reputation will become ever more important. Smart communicators are already pushing beyond measuring outputs and outtakes, and learning to measure the feelings, perceptions, and relationships that they generate. What people think of you, how they perceive your actions, and what they do as a result of those perceptions are truly the metrics of the future.

Increasingly, organizations will need to use Grunig's methodology (and that of those who will enhance and expand on his research) to measure their credibility and the trust that their actions engender. The challenge will be how to get accurate opinions from an increasingly fragmented and independent constituency.

The biggest complaint we hear about relationship measures is the length of survey questionnaires; people just don't want to spend the time and effort necessary to complete a questionnaire comprehensive enough to measure relationships. When you think about it, however, survey responses are a rather crude way to determine someone's feelings about things. The use of new metrics will make it increasingly easier to tease relationship-related answers out of people, perhaps by measuring facial response, blood pressure, body language, eye movements, or some other type of biometric.

Relationship measurement will benefit from the development of new and more powerful tools. You'll see increased sophistication in text-mining software and natural language programming. These tools will soon be able to pull meaning out of that big bucket o' words called new media, and communicators will be able to automatically determine whether their messages are going out and just how they are being positioned. Of course, quantifying and manipulating all that data will be a challenge. Who knows what new techniques will become feasible as the rapid growth of computing power continues?

Another interesting notion is a system or program that could extend media content analysis to include the concepts behind Grunig's relationship theory. Imagine being able to pull from the media all the various ways that journalists and those they interview refer to trust or commitment. Or being able to analyze blog comments and rate them on any of Grunig and Hon's relationship components. If we could express all our results in terms of the fundamental components of relationships, then we'd have a truly integrated approach, and our research would be vastly more valuable than it is today.

Additionally, measurement will become more and more focused on the mobile consumer. We will get more and more of our news and information from cell phones, PDAs, iPods and other mobile devices. These devices will become critical drivers of the relationships that companies have with consumers.

Increasingly, we will move to a more integrated approach, measuring the impact and outcomes of those outputs we've been so fond of counting. The real challenge will be to figure out what to do with the information. In a communications environment that changes faster every day and continuously provides us with new media and ways to communicate, the accountable communicator will have no shortage of data on which to base his or her decisions. The key to success will be to interpret that data correctly.

Glossary

*Say, oh wise man, how have you come to such knowledge?
Because I was never ashamed to confess my ignorance and ask
others.*
　　　　　　　　　　　　　　　　—Johann Gottfried von Herder

A large part of measurement is about language. In fact (to use a
concept adapted from John Gray's "Men Are from Mars, Women
Are from Venus," www.marsvenus.com), it is about the two different languages used by Martians and Venusians. Venusians
are people who tend to think and speak in a style most readily
expressed by words—words like messages, target audiences, and
relationships. In the business world, Venusians tend to work in
communications. Martians tend to think and speak in a style most
readily expressed by numbers—numbers like ROI, revenue, and
quarterly results. And in business, Martians tend to be in management. And so it often happens that Venusians have a difficult time
communicating in a fashion that Martians can understand—and
vice versa. One of the benefits of measurement is that it allows
communications and management to talk to each other.

Over time, researchers and measurement experts have
developed their own terms that can frequently be confusing
to the person who is new to the measurement process. This
Glossary has been adapted from the Institute for Public Relations'

Dictionary of Measurement Terms, edited and compiled by Dr. Donald Stacks of the University of Miami, and fully downloadable from the IPR's website, www.instituteforpr.org. Italic terms in the definitions indicate cross references.

advertising value equivalent (AVE)—An unproven and suspect measure of PR value based on calculating the *column inches* of a story and determining the equivalent cost of buying the same size advertising space in the same publication.

baseline or benchmark—An initial measurement against which subsequent measures are compared.

benchmarking or benchmark study—A measurement technique that involves having an organization learn something about its own practices and/or the practices of selected others, and then compares these practices. Research that establishes a *benchmark* (see).

causal relationship—A relationship between variables in which a change in one variable forces, produces, or brings about a change in another variable.

census—A collection of data from every person or object in a population.

circulation—Number of copies of a publication as distributed. Not usually the same as the number actually read, but as a practical matter, synonymous with *opportunities to see, impressions*, and *reach*.

column inches—The total length of an printed article if it were all one column, measured in inches.

communication(s) audit—A systematic review and analysis of how effectively an organization communicates with all of its major internal and external audiences.

content analysis—An informal research methodology and measurement tool that systematically tracks messages (written, spoken, broadcast) and translates them into quantifiable form by defining message categories and specified units of analysis.

correlation—A statistical test that examines the relationships between variables.

cost per message communicated (CPMC)— Similar to *CPM*, but adjusted for the number of messages that actually appeared in the media coverage. Note that here "M" refers to "message."

cost per thousand (CPM)—Cost per impression or cost per person reached. As used in advertising, it is the cost of advertising for each 1,000 homes reached. Note that here "M" refers to "thousand," as M is the Roman numeral for one thousand.

dashboard—A technique for simplifying data reporting by displaying a small number of important summary measures together in one location. Like an automotive dashboard, a PR dashboard includes only those measures most critical for assessing the progress or health of a program or company.

demographic analysis—The analysis of a population in terms of social, political, economic, and geographic subgroups (for example, age, sex, income level, race, educational level, place of residence, occupation).

demographic data—Data that differentiates between groups of people by social, political, economic, and geographic characteristics.

editorial or earned media—(1) The content of a publication written by a journalist, as distinct from advertising content, which is determined by an advertiser; (2) An article expressing the editorial policy of a publication on a matter of interest (also known as a "leader" or "leading article"); (3) Space in a publication bought by an advertiser that includes journalistic copy intended to make the reader think it originates from an independent source (also known as an "advertorial").

focus group methodology—An informal research technique that uses a group discussion approach to gain an in-depth understanding of a client, object, or product; is not generalizable to other focus groups or populations.

frequency—A descriptive statistic that represents the number of objects being counted (for example, number of advertisements, number of people who attend an event, number of media release pickups).

gross rating points (GRP)—A measure most broadcast advertisers use to determine the extent to which their advertising messages have penetrated a specific audience. The GRP of a show or ad represents the percentage of the total audience who actually viewed it.

impressions—Opportunities to see an article or message generated by the total audited circulation of a publication. For example, if *The Wall Street Journal* has an audited circulation of 1.5 million, one article in that paper generates 1.5 million impressions or opportunities to see the story. Two articles generate 3 million impressions, and so on. *Opportunities to see, circulation, impressions,* and *reach* are synonymous.

key message—A specific statement or concept that an organization is trying to communicate about itself. A common general goal of PR is to get key messages into media coverage. A key message ought to be unique to your organization and it must be something that a journalist is likely to print, for example, "Company X provides the best customer service in the industry," or, "Company Y's product is of the highest quality."

message content—(1) The verbal, visual, and audio elements of a message; (2) The material from which *content analyses* are conducted; (3) A *trend analysis* factor that measures what planned messages are actually contained in the media.

message content analysis—Analysis of media coverage of a client, product, or topic on key issues.

message strength—How strongly a message about a client, product, or topic was communicated.

objectives—A clearly defined set of goals that are in line with overall strategic marketing, sales, and corporate objectives.

omnibus survey—An all-purpose national consumer *poll* usually conducted on a regular schedule (once a week or every other week) by major market research firms; also called a "piggyback" or "shared-cost" *survey*.

opportunities to see (OTS)—A number equal to the total audited circulation of a publication. *Opportunities to see, circulation, impressions,* and *reach* are synonymous.

outcomes—Quantifiable changes in attitudes, behaviors, or opinions that occur as end results of a PR program.

outputs—The physical products of a PR program; anything that is published or directly produced by the public relations team. Outputs can be articles, white papers, speaking engagements, the number of times a spokesperson is quoted, specific messages communicated, specific positioning on an important issue, or any number of quantifiable items.

outtakes—What members of your target audiences take away from your program—the messages, perceptions and understandings that your program has generated. *Outtakes* are the perceptions generated by your *outputs.*

poll—(1) A form of *survey* research that focuses more on immediate behavior than attitudes; (2) A very short *survey*-like method using a *questionnaire* that asks only very short and closed-ended questions.

positioning—How an organization is perceived on broad industry characteristics, such as leadership, innovation, employer of choice, neighbor of choice, and so forth.

program or **campaign**—The planning, execution, and evaluation of a public relations plan of action aimed at solving a problem.

psychographic research—Research focusing on nondemographic traits and characteristics, such as personality type, lifestyle, social roles, values, attitudes, and beliefs.

public—(1) A group of people whose behavior may have consequences for an organization or who are affected by the consequences of organizational decisions; (2) A group of people from which a public relations *campaign* or *program* selects specific *targeted audiences* in an attempt to influence behavior or attitudes regarding a company, product, issue, or individual.

qualitative research—Studies that are somewhat to totally subjective, but nevertheless in-depth, using a probing, open-ended response format.

quantitative research—Studies that are highly objective and projectable, using closed-ended, forced-choice *questionnaires*; research that relies heavily on statistics and numerical measures.

questionnaire—A measurement instrument that uses questions to collect data for the analysis of some aspect of a group. May be employed through the mail, Internet, in person, or via the telephone. May be both closed-ended and open-ended, but typically employs more closed-ended questions. A *questionnaire* is the instrument used in a *survey*.

reach—The scope or range of distribution and thus coverage that a given communication product has in a targeted audience group. The total audited circulation of a publication. In broadcasting, the net unduplicated (also called "deduplicated") radio or TV audience for programs. *Opportunities to see, circulation, impressions,* and *reach* are synonymous.

reach demographics—Reach into specific demographic segments, determined using data from one of the generally accepted sources such as SRDS or Simmons.

response rate—The number of respondents who actually complete an interview or reply to some request, usually expressed as a percentage of all those who received the interview or request.

sample—A group of people or objects chosen from a larger population.

share of ink (SOI)—The percentage of total press coverage or *opportunities to see* devoted to a particular client or product.

share of voice (SOV)—The percentage of total radio or television coverage or *opportunities to see* devoted to a particular client or product; also known as "share of coverage."

survey—The process of gathering data from a *sample* of a population. The instrument used in a survey is called a *questionnaire*.

target audience—A specific subset of a total audience, differentiated by some characteristic or attribute (for example, sports fishermen), that is the specific focus of a marketing or public relations effort.

targeted gross rating points (TGRP)—*Gross rating points* (GRP) with respect to a particular group or *target audience*.

tone—Trend and *content analysis* factor that measures how a *target audience* feels about the client, product, or topic; typically defined as positive, neutral/balanced, or negative.

trend analysis—Tracking of performance over the course of a PR campaign or program. A *survey* method whereby a topic or subject is examined over a period of time through repeated surveys of independently selected *samples*.

Appendix 1:
The Grunig
Relationship Survey

The easiest and most reliable methodology for assessing the state of relationships between organizations and their publics is a set of survey questions developed by James Grunig, Larissa Grunig, and Linda Hon at the University of Maryland. The development of this survey tool was motivated by the authors' search for a way to assess the long-term value of public relations to an organization. Convinced that, "the fundamental goal of public relations is to build and then enhance on-going or long-term relationships with an organization's key constituencies," they set out to develop a method to measure the health of relationships.

The results of this effort are presented in "Guidelines for Measuring Relationships in Public Relations" by Linda Hon and James Grunig, a paper that can be downloaded at no charge from the IPR website or at www.measuresofsuccess.com. I encourage you to read at least the first several sections of this paper. Not only does it present in detail the ideas and research behind the Grunig Relationship Survey, but it also makes an eloquent statement about the nature and importance of relationships to the practice of public relations. Much of this book builds directly on the work presented there.

Hon and Grunig's research identified six distinct and individually measurable relationship components: control mutuality, trust, commitment, satisfaction, exchange relationship, and communal relationship. They tested a series of agree-or-disagree statements that measure these individual components. This set of questions, which in this book we call the Grunig Relationship Survey, has been thoroughly tested and shown to be an extremely effective measure of how customers or members perceive their relationships with an organization. One of the components measured by this survey, trust, has been the subject of much research and is the subject of Chapter 6 in this book.

Typical agree-or-disagree statements from the Grunig Relationship Survey include:

- I am happy with this organization.

- Whenever this organization makes an important decision, I know it will be concerned about people like me.

- This organization can be relied on to keep its promises.

- I believe that this organization takes the opinions of people like me into account when making decisions.

- I feel very confident about this organization's skills.

The full list of questions to measure each of the six relationship components can be found in the Hon and Grunig paper mentioned above. For more detail on administering the survey, see this follow-up paper by Jim Grunig: "Qualitative Methods for Assessing Relationships Between Organizations and Publics" (also available at the IPR website, www.instituteforpr.org).

The challenge in using the Grunig survey is that few organizations have the resources or budget to conduct such an extensive survey. A questionnaire comprehensive enough to measure all six relationship components is lengthy. It can take a long time to administer and for respondents to complete. In fact, that's the biggest complaint we hear about using it.

However (as Jim Grunig has pointed out in personal correspondence), you don't have to use all eight or so items for each concept. The Hon and Grunig paper includes a shorter list of items that can be used to keep the questionnaire briefer without sacrificing reliability. You may decide that such an abbreviated version is more appropriate for your situation. If so, pay careful attention to which relationship components you wish to measure and which questions you need to ask to do so.

Increasingly, organizations are selecting two or three of the Hon and Grunig statements and incorporating them into reputation and relationship surveys that they conduct by phone or mail or online. The most useful statements are those that tease out the weaknesses in a relationship. These are the "reverse" statements such as, "This is an organization that tends to throw its weight around," or "This is an organization that you need to keep an eye on."

An example of this technique's advantages was a recent survey of subscribers to a utility, in which respondents responded positively to generic questions about the organization's reputation. But when pressed to agree or disagree with statements on whether the organization could be trusted, the survey revealed that there was a high level of suspicion about the utility's recent actions. As a result, the PR department was able to address those concerns and rectify the situation.

The most reliable way to administer the Grunig Relationship Survey is to conduct in-depth phone interviews, but not every organization has the means or resources to do this. There are several alternatives, of which online surveys are most popular. Online surveys suffer from the drawback of employing a self-selecting sample (only those interested in the topic are likely to complete the questionnaire), but the trade-offs in terms of cost and timing are hard to beat. They are particularly effective in measuring relationships with members of an organization that are all on a listserve of some sort (see Chapter 13, "Measuring Relationships with Members").

Appendix 2
Measurement Resources

Books on Public Relations and Public Relations Research

Using Research In Public Relations: Applications to Program Management, by Glen M. Broom and David M. Dozier (Englewood Cliffs, NJ: Prentice Hall, 1990, 1996). ISBN: 0139391665.

Primer of Public Relations Research, by Don W. Stacks (New York: The Guilford Press, 2002). ISBN: 1572307269.

Public Relations Research for Planning and Evaluation, by Walter K. Lindenmann (available from the IPR website, www.instituteforpr.org).

Excellence in Public Relations and Communication Management, by James E. Grunig and Larissa A. Grunig (Hillsdale, NJ: Lawrence Erlbaum Associates Inc., 1992).

Excellent Public Relations and Effective Organizations, by James E. Grunig, Larissa A. Grunig, and David M. Dozier (Hillsdale, NJ: Lawrence Erlbaum Associates Inc., 2002).

Two useful resources for qualitative and quantitative research techniques (both available from the Advertising Research Foundation, 432 Park Avenue South, New York, NY 10016):

Guidelines for the Public Use of Market and Opinion Research.

The ARF Guidelines Handbook: A Compendium of Guidelines to Good Advertising, Marketing and Media Research Practice.

Books on Media Content Analysis

Primer of Public Relations Research, by Don W. Stacks (New York: The Guilford Press, 2002). ISBN: 1572307269.

Media Relations Measurement, by Ralf Leinemann and Elena Baikaltseva (Aldershot, Hampshire, England: Gower, 2004). ISBN: E0566086506.

References for Trust Research and Measurement

Measuring Organizational Trust: A Diagnostic Survey and International Indicator by Pamela Shockley-Zalabak, Kathleen Ellis, and Ruggero Cesaria (San Francisco: IABC Research Foundation, 2000). ISBN: 1888015225.

From the IPR website, www.instituteforpr.org:

Can There Be Just One Trust? A Cross-Disciplinary Identification of Trust Definitions and Measurement by Marcia Watson.

Guidelines for Measuring Relationships in Public Relations by Linda Childers Hon and James E. Grunig.

Guidelines for Measuring Trust in Organizations by Katie Paine, in association with Linda Hon and Jim Grunig.

Restoring Trust in Business: Models for Action by The Public Relations Coalition.

Websites

www.measuresofsuccess.com KDPaine & Partners' public relations measurement resource center; includes guides to vendors and many free papers.

www.themeasurementstandard.com KDPaine & Partners' monthly newsletter on public relations measurement.

http://kdpaine.blogs.com/ Katie Delahaye Paine's public relations measurement blog.

www.instituteforpr.org The site of the Institute for Public Relations; includes many free papers and resources.

About the Author

Katie Delahaye Paine is the founder and CEO of KDPaine & Partners, LLC. In the relentless pursuit of quantitative and qualitative measures of success, she and her employees have read and analyzed millions of news articles, blogs, newsgroup postings, and internal communications, and have conducted hundreds of thousands of interviews. Most recently her endeavors have been focused on social media measurement as well as providing cost-effective measurement programs for nonprofits, small businesses, and government agencies.

Katie is a founder and former chair of the Institute for Public Relations Special Commission on Measurement and Evaluation. She served as the U.S. liaison to the European Standards Task Force to set international standards for media evaluation. She writes a regular column for *PR News* on corporate image and crisis communications, and contributes to *Communications World*, *PR Week*, *Business Marketing*, and *New Hampshire Magazine*.

An accomplished speaker, Katie frequently lectures to conferences and universities including The American Strategic Management Institute, the Public Relations Society of America, the International Association of Business Communicators, and the Institute for International Research. Katie began and still writes the world's first measurement blog (http://kdpaine.blogs.com) and publishes *The Measurement Standard* newsletter (www.themeasurementstandard.com).

Printed in the United States
119056LV00003B/244-351/A